The idea of group projects in textile art is nothing new: people have come together to sew for centuries, and quilters often work communally on large projects such as 'story quilts'. But recently the trend has increased in popularity – artists regularly get together to share ideas and work sociably, from simple one-to-one collaborations with friends to ambitious community projects.

In this fascinating book, well-known textile artists Cas Holmes and Anne Kelly present an invaluable guide to working collaboratively, in both small and large groups. They provide useful information on setting up groups, finding venues, establishing ground rules and working methods, and staging group exhibitions, plus a wealth of practical inspiration for ways to work together – working on one project at the same time, swapping pieces between different people, creating different variations on a theme, developing work by means of joint sketchbooks, and even working postally or online. They also demonstrate how working with other artists can have a positive influence on your own personal work. The authors have been involved in a very productive collaboration for several years, *Resonant Textiles,* and also regularly devise and run community events and gallery exhibitions, both together and separately.

Illustrated with many examples of work produced collaboratively, this thought-provoking book will help you connect with other artists and take your own work beyond the personal.

Connected Cloth

Connected Cloth

Creating Collaborative Textile Projects

Cas Holmes & Anne Kelly

BATSFORD

First published in the United Kingdom in 2013 by
Batsford
10 Southcombe Street
London
W14 0RA

An imprint of Anova Books Company Ltd

ISBN 978 1 84994 043 6

A CIP catalogue for this book is available from the British Library.

22 21 20 19 18 17 16 15 14 13
10 9 8 7 6 5 4 3 2 1

Reproduction by Rival Colour Ltd, UK
Printed and bound by Craft Print International Ltd, Singapore

This book can be ordered direct from the publisher at
www.anovabooks.com, or try your local bookshop.

Page 1, left: *Beetle Badge*
(Anne Kelly).
Page 1, right: *Wild Rose*
(Cas Holmes).
Page 2: *Winter Sun* (detail)
(Cas Holmes).
Below: *Norfolk Weeds* (detail)
(Cas Holmes and Anne Kelly).

Contents

Introduction

Our relationship with cloth is both personal and intimate, yet it is one shared globally. We dress our families in the morning to 'face the world' and pull bedclothes over us at night to sleep. *Connected Cloth* explores our relationship with textiles and their use as a collaborative creative medium. Most contemporary practitioners are women, and this has been the case historically. Women have made the garments for the family to wear, quilts for the bed and various household items for decoration and use. Bone needles used by *Homo sapiens* over 40,000 years ago provide historical evidence that even then we clothed ourselves by necessity, for warmth and comfort.

The terms associated with cloth are familiar and form part of our daily exchange with others. We talk about 'patching things up' as a metaphor for repairing 'frayed' relationships, or a 'stitch in time' to repair a broken item. Activities such as sewing, knitting and quilting long have been, and still are, shared experiences, providing a chance for individuals to exchange skills, to meet and to talk. This need to share ideas and collaborate remains important for today's practitioners as they continue to develop textile techniques and media to create new works.

The concept for this book developed out of the successful and productive exhibiting and curation partnership between the two authors, Resonant Textiles. It also builds on the aspects of communal textiles and the community briefly discussed in 'Sharing', the final chapter in *The Found Object in Textile Art* (Cas Holmes, Batsford, 2010). Through sharing and exchanging ideas, both as artists and teachers, we recognize the value of working with other people and the connections textiles can make with the world around us.

When we discuss collaboration, we are interested in the different approaches to the textile exchange between artists, within groups and at an international level, where personal and cultural interchange can be both stimulating and challenging. We look at how such a sharing of skills, ideas and techniques can connect cloth to a given space and to people and create a dialogue between makers. We explore different approaches to the creative process, reflecting a wide range of artists' interactions, from community projects to environmental works, as well as collaborations exploring personal and cultural identities.

In the first section of this book, 'Resonant Textiles', we look at the specific advantages of working collaboratively. The challenges of working to a theme and approaches to developing processes and ideas are discussed alongside the practicalities of managing our work professionally as artists, in our very busy lives. As part of the process of 'connection', you will, as you read through this book, find practical suggestions and information concerning various aspects of collaboration, for both exhibitions and group events, as well as for working in education and the community. This includes examples of collaborative work in museums and galleries, as well as work by internationally renowned artists in the UK and abroad.

Cas Holmes and Anne Kelly
2013

Right: *Whole Moth Tablecloth* (detail) (Anne Kelly).

Far right: *The Lea* (detail) (Cas Holmes).

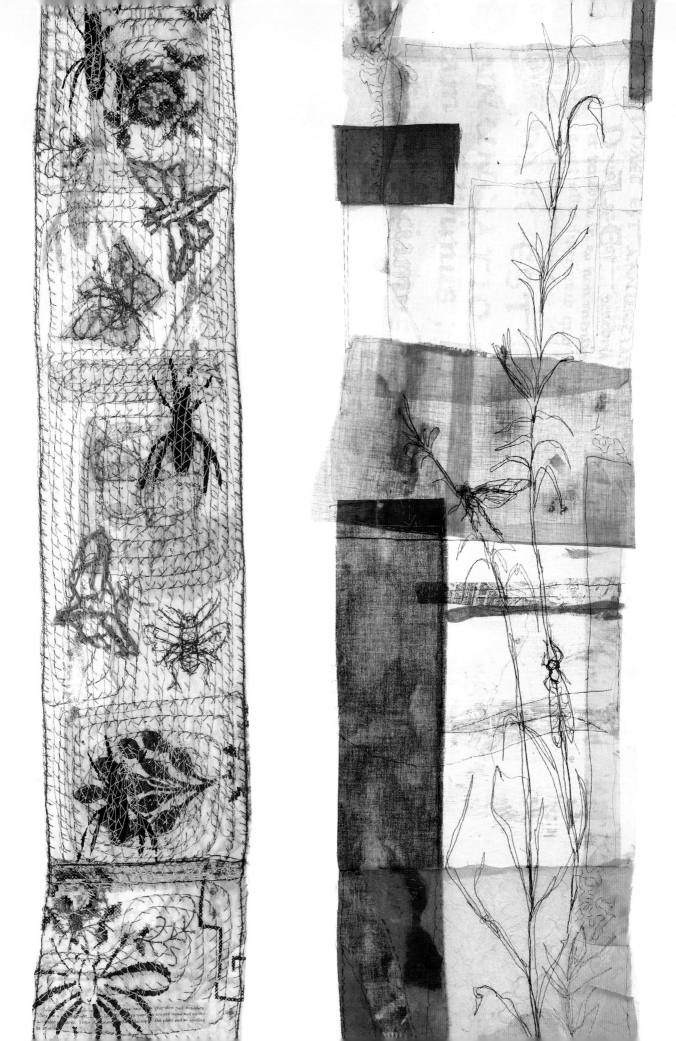

1 Resonant Textiles

Connections and Collaborations

In 2008, a chance encounter at West Dean College inspired the beginning of a collaboration: an ongoing project called 'Resonant Textiles'. The authors of this book hold workshops in each other's studios and meet regularly as a means to cross-fertilize ideas and techniques and to counteract what is at times the artist's greatest enemy – isolation. In exchanging our ideas, aided by these 'development days', in which we spend time together drawing, gathering resources and visiting exhibitions, we develop and critique our work and challenge our expectations. Working together requires commitment, as we also practise as individual artists, so getting to the right place at the same time can be a challenge. This cross-exchange also takes place by email, which enables us to find new approaches to sharing ideas and resources as we develop projects, and also to explore exhibiting possibilities.

When we research potential projects and exhibitions, a number of factors influences our decisions about what we want to do and how we want to be involved. Most crucially, potential projects need to fit with the ideas behind our work: the exploration of the local landscape, places visited and everyday life. In addition, the nature of our work is labour-intensive and we also need time to develop our ideas. Any decision on a new project is very much influenced by our individual availability, as well as other time and financial constraints.

We both feel that our experience in education is a valuable component of our collaboration which also feeds a larger purpose – that of passing on our experience and skills to our students.

From our first meeting together, we established a good working relationship, bolstered by some basic starting points and approaches to the collaboration. In this chapter, we will look in further detail at the work and methods we use and make practical suggestions for setting up your own collaborations. This is supported by visual examples of projects and suggestions of themes you can look at in developing your own textile practice.

Previous pages: *Norfolk Weeds* (detail) (Cas Holmes and Anne Kelly).
Right: *Seed Bird Map* (Cas Holmes and Anne Kelly).

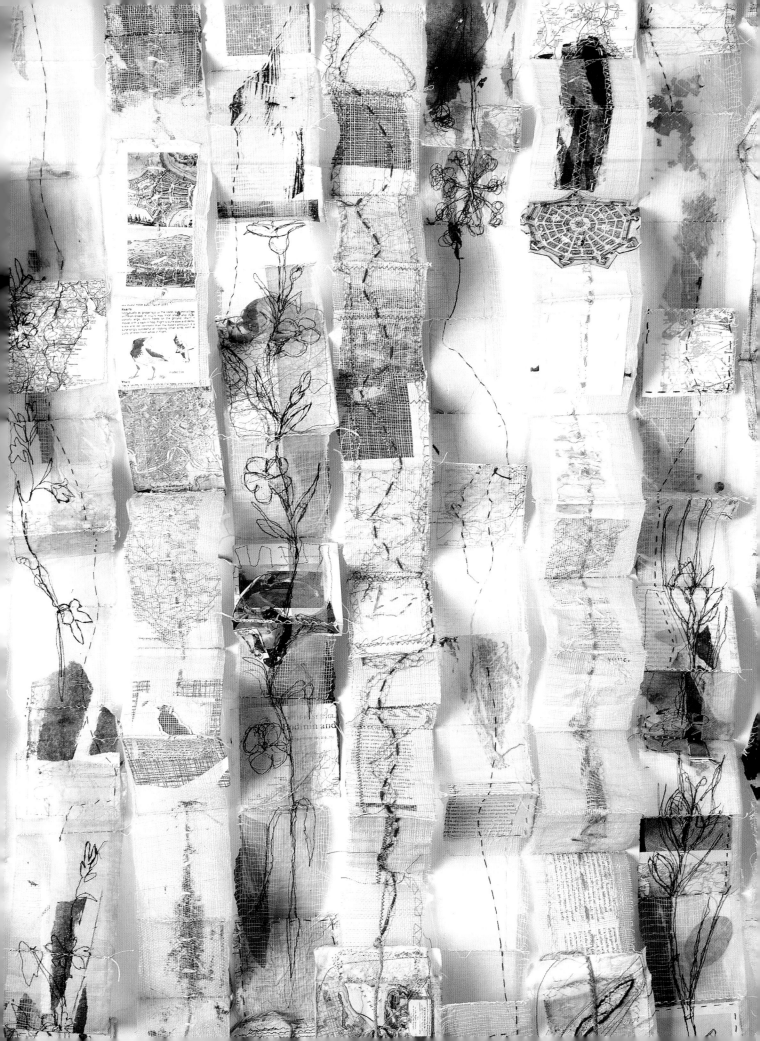

Beginnings

We each have our own approaches to working, so part of the challenge of collaboration is finding out what themes and ideas we share and respecting what is different. Some of the experiences we discuss here as part of the creative process might echo your own thoughts: the need to find time and space to work, the value of recording and making drawings and, most of all, being honest in what we find works or (more often than not) what doesn't. Having another person's opinion is a very important part of the collaboration; it takes the 'personal' away from the decision-making process and also helps to channel our discoveries into new areas.

We use discarded items and vintage and waste material no longer considered useful. Old and forgotten textiles, found objects and paper have a history, and this is a shared focus for the work. As part of the process of making, we explore and exchange ideas as well as materials. Broken down, torn and cut, the fragments and layers mark the passing of time, while the rituals of making (cutting paper, gathering materials, machining, sewing) act as part of the narrative of the work, creating new textiles from old. The environmental impact of producing work from waste materials in recessionary times is also explored, as it fits into the current trend of 'upcycling'.

Right: *Shared Paths* (Cas Holmes). Detail of 'Lost', based on a poster attached to a lamppost in a park.

Far right: *Under the Pomegranate Tree* (detail) (Anne Kelly). This detail shows the central panel, with hand and machine stitch.

Research, drawing and recording

Drawing and recording are crucial to our work and always form part of our studio days and times when we visit exhibitions and galleries. Our basic approach is based on what we observe, combined with our personal experience of both the subject and the found objects and materials we use to inform that experience. Our sketchbooks reflect our interests, containing personal narratives relating how we observe the world around us and informing our individual practice as well as our joint projects. Collage, paint and even direct stitching in the sketchbooks all develop into ideas for paper and fabric collages, using found images and waste materials joined together by hand and machine.

The approach that we have adopted to drawing is flexible and we have undertaken sketchbook work in a variety of settings.

- **Domestic** – while working in our studios/homes – mostly from observation, we have found the seasonal changes in our gardens deeply inspirational; alternatively, small collections of domestic objects, such as a sewing kit or food items, can be useful starting points.

- **Galleries and other public settings** – a small book in your pocket is a useful tool to aid the observation of various elements of interest in an exhibition, museum or gallery, where you sometimes cannot use a camera. You also need to be aware of further restrictions, as the use of paints or wet media is sometimes not allowed where there may be a risk to the artwork or collections. Coloured pencils or written notes on colour are useful in these situations.

- **Information-gathering sessions** include visits to places of interest, such as local parks or woodland, and found imagery, objects and papers gathered as we go about our daily lives.

The importance of drawing and sketchbook work cannot be overstated. Drawing reinforces our observation and plays a role in articulating and sharing our ideas. It is an essential tool for research, aids the development of images and themes, and leads to the creation of new work as part of the collaborative process. In discussing our work with students or in 'meet the artist' sessions, we always refer to drawing as a useful, even essential, tool which helps us develop our artistic ideas.

Below: Sketchbook showing development of ideas, including notes, text and bird sketches (Anne Kelly).

Right: Pages from our 'Garden Sketchbooks' showing found paper, stitch and collage (Top: Anne Kelly, bottom Cas Holmes).

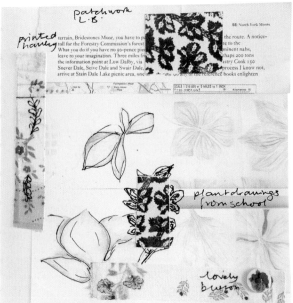

for Seed
Bird
Map

professor — you get a monument for that?
Talnotry is a class B campsite, and there is
forest trail 482-716 of rough walking for 4
miles over uneven but interesting country. The

Deer Range with   and a

Great Dixter
August '09

Above: Small research sketchbooks, demonstrating different approaches and marks used to document the world around us. (Top: Anne Kelly; bottom: Cas Holmes).

Left: Sketches from our 'Garden Sketchbooks' incorporating fabric and found papers (Top: Anne Kelly; bottom: Cas Holmes).

Top: Location shots on Tunbridge Wells Common, Kent. Left: Cas Holmes checking out a 'lost dog' sign on a lamppost; right: the sign itself. **Bottom:** Sketchbook showing layered drawings of snow on branches for winter-themed work (Cas Holmes).

A sketchbook for collaboration

Here are some basic rules of thumb when starting a sketchbook for collaboration:

1. Choose a small book that is easy to carry.

2. Use a pencil case containing a range of drawing materials and a small watercolour set and brush. A glue stick is also useful for sticking in notes, sections from information leaflets, tickets and so on.

3. Start with a common image or theme that you can each interpret in different ways – our first joint sketchbook focused on the theme of our gardens and the changing elements in these personal spaces.

4. Don't be too precious about it – it is meant as a workbook, not a series of finished studies, although some sketchbooks may become that.

5. Take a camera with you when visiting new places or on your travels in general; you never know what you may see.

6. Always review and reflect on your work – you can add to the sketchbook or journal as your work progresses.

Sharing and exchanging drawing skills can take place in informal settings. We often sketch with other groups and attend classes. Adult-education classes are a good place in which to learn and improve your drawing. You could also consider setting up your own local drawing group or signing up for one of the many forums for online exchange.

Below: Anne Kelly working on location in Cas Holmes's garden.

The studio/workspace

It is essential to have a workspace in which you can connect with your practice. This may be a purpose-built studio or only a tabletop or a shared space, but you need somewhere to create and develop ideas. We are fortunate in being able to set aside small workspaces in our homes and then, when we get together, the kitchen and other living spaces supplement our studios as places for working.

Artist Jo Budd gathers imagery and influences from her native East Anglia where, for the last six years, she has worked from her purpose-built studio, looking over water meadows in rural North Suffolk:

My studio space ... is my sacred space, dedicated only to one thing. I love my 'journey' to work down the garden. This is a little mental separation from the rest of the 'noise' of life, and preparation for a different mental state. Surrounded by garden and looking over marshland pastures, the peaceful and serene atmosphere makes working there a wonderful experience. Since I have had this space the work has poured out, more ideas than I have time to play with. What I have produced in it is both a celebration of my surroundings and an expression of liberation, which this space makes me feel.

Jo Budd, Extracts from notes for the V&A commission.

Right: Jo Budd looking at her works *Male/Winter* (on wall) and *Female/Summer* (on floor) in progress in her studio.

Your workspace is an extension of your sketchbook; it is where you develop your ideas and make notes. These are some of the things you may need when setting up a place in which to work, whether in your home or outside it:

- **A table at a good working height**, possibly for use with a sewing machine and for drawing (it might well be a shared table, or perhaps a board to fit on an existing surface).

- **A noticeboard or pinboard for samples and work in progress**; you can create an artificial or temporary place to hang work by attaching plain fabric (such as calico) to picture rails or battens and suspending this on hooks from the wall or other supporting structure.

- **An additional storage space for fabrics and papers**, such as a good set of drawers, a cupboard with shelves or even baskets and small boxes.

- **A place for wet/messy work** – this may well be in an additional space or you might just have plenty of plastic table covers to protect communal areas.

Safe practice is an important consideration: clearly label storage containers, ensure you clean up thoroughly if a space has a shared use, and check you have adequate protection and are aware of the health and safety requirements of any materials you are using.

We are aware that not everyone has the advantage of a separate space to set aside for work, but with a little creative thinking you can create a space for textile art. Many of the items discussed are portable and can be folded away, and simple storage in the form of boxes or baskets can be carried to your workspace. We both have portable kits for working in different places, such as the garden on a lovely day, or to take with us when working away from home.

Below: Cas Holmes's studio. **Right:** Anne Kelly's studio.
Our workspaces reveal our joint interest in collecting objects and images for inspiration. Clever storage helps us to locate these finds easily.

Themes and inspiration

How we work, shared ideas, different approaches

Working on themes and discussing ideas helps to give structure to our work. The practice of textile art is richly diverse and, by focusing on a given starting point, something as simple as looking at our garden paths allows us to develop a range of approaches. What we learn from one piece of work can then be carried over into the next. There is always a fear of failure but, more importantly, we are also open to discovery. Our starting point is always observation and discussion, and the themes or sequences we develop for collaboration reflect both individual and shared experiences.

Below: *Seed Bird Map* (Cas Holmes and Anne Kelly). Top: Sketchbook (Cas Holmes) showing development of ideas; middle: stitched strip by Anne Kelly; bottom: work in progress by Cas Holmes.

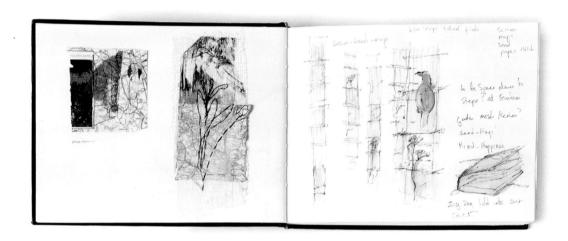

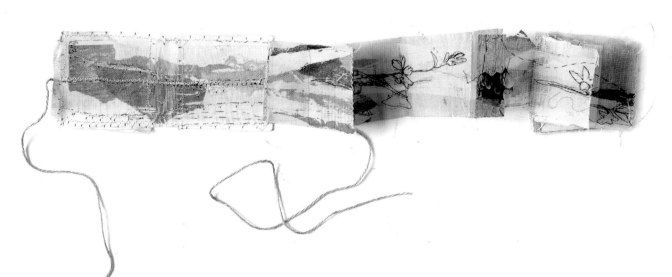

Cas's approach

My work is based on observations and memories; I live in a house that edges a park, bringing the 'urban' and 'nature' together. My interest is in the open landscape, marks made by man in the earth, reflections in water, the changing seasons in my garden and the places where the 'domestic' meets the outside spaces. I am influenced by the ideals of *wabi-sabi* (see below): things often overlooked, details, worn surfaces and beauty that can be found in the transience of things imperfect, impermanent and incomplete. Materials include fragments of domestic textiles, pages of old books, discarded materials and objects that have personal associations or that conjure up memories. This ongoing dialogue with the material brings its own history, which is woven into the work. Sketchbooks contain drawings and notes as a means to sum up the emotional response to what I see, as well as reflecting my concerns about the land, both intimate and global. Working on several pieces at once, I find that one idea will 'feed' another, giving me time to reflect and get to the essence of what I want to achieve. Embarking on a new theme or project fills me with anxiety, but the passion for expression is constant, and I have learnt that if a piece does not work, it should be cut up and re-used.

Right: *Lea Valley* (detail) (Cas Holmes). This piece combines an old sewing pattern with photographs of plants in the Lea Valley, with machine and hand stitching.

Wabi-sabi is the quintessential Japanese aesthetic; it is a beauty of things imperfect, impermanent and incomplete. It is a beauty of things unconventional. The two separate words, *wabi* and *sabi*, have related but different meanings. *Wabi* is the kind of beauty which, paradoxically, comes from having just the right kind of imperfection, such as an asymmetrical ceramic bowl, reflecting the handmade craftsmanship, as opposed to a bowl which is perfect, but soulless and machine-made. *Sabi* is the kind of beauty that can come only with age, such as the patina and wear on a piece of carved wood.

A wabi-sabi *lifestyle where nothing is perfect allows us the space, time and freedom to live in the moment and enjoy and engage with being creative. It's about coming up with new ideas, finding different ways to solve problems and bringing something new into existence.*

www.wabisabi.org.uk

Anne's approach

I am a collector of vintage fabric, paper and ephemera, using collage, stitch and photographic and print processes to create a range of work. Travel, memory and vintage imagery from a variety of sources inspire my work, which has been described as being like 'small worlds' made from what at first appear to be disparate collage elements. These worlds are often botanical in subject matter and eventually develop into larger, more narrative works. The components of each work are assembled and reassembled, using sketchbooks and digital imagery. Often it can be a small scrap or remnant of fabric that inspires a whole piece. I frequently return to images of birds and explore how they fit into different environments. I am inspired by naive folk art, textiles and the works of artists who are self-taught as opposed to 'arts-trained', sometimes referred to as 'outsider artists'. My studio is a repository for vintage fabrics, sewing items, books old and new, and art materials. I like to find a use for random pieces of fabric, old sections of garments and other detritus and refashion them into new artworks. It is the kind of work that is easily transportable and that I can return to frequently. Commissioned works are a large part of my practice, and I use the same method of construction and collage to complete them.

Below: *Sophia Bianca* (detail) (Anne Kelly). Collage using vintage domestic fabrics, book pages and machine- and hand-stitching.

Shared approaches

We share a love of the natural world and our interaction with it. The space outside our front doors can be a rich source of inspiration and point of reference. Simple everyday objects and views take on a more personal meaning and can have resonance with the viewer of the work. Starting points include sketchbooks, photographs and drawings, and ideas evolving from these are exchanged as part of our practice.

We are attracted to, and identify with, the narrative and historical qualities of domestic materials and found objects as a creative resource, which we use in new contexts. We tend to have a number of projects, including teaching and commissioned works, on the go at any one time. We are often asked 'how long does it take?' and the answer to this is 'quite a long time'.

In what follows, we refer to ourselves in the third person to identify references to our individual approaches more easily.

Above: *Domestic Mapping* (Cas Holmes [top right and bottom left] and Anne Kelly [top left and bottom right]). The full work is composed of 16 pieces in total, eight pieces by Cas and eight pieces by Anne. Each piece is 35cm (13¾in) square. The pieces are displayed in various square arrangements (2 x 2 or 4 x 4), depending on location. Each piece uses a tea towel as its base cloth. At this stage of our collaboration we were working together on prints, and exchanged our prints with each other.

Changing surfaces and making marks

We both use colour and make marks with inks, dyes and
paint and with transfer, a heritage from our fine-art training.
Cas prepares found fabric and paper surfaces specifically
by layering them with paste, dye and paint on to a plastic
surface. When the layers are dried, they are removed from the
plastic and are then machine- and hand-stitched. Cas leaves
open space in her pieces, using a 'painterly' mark in response
to the found surfaces.

Anne uses printed fabric and found items, sometimes
additionally painted and pinned together before stitching to
hold the base layers together. Mark-making with print and
brush is used to build up surface texture. Anne's pieces are
densely worked and directly respond to the colours of the
cloth she finds.

We both use old domestic fabrics because of their link
to women and the home. These finds often have a worn
patina from handling and interesting references to pattern
and colour, which can be transformed into new surfaces for
textiles. Paper has different qualities, allowing us to transfer
our drawings more directly and simply to the work. The many
varieties of paper about, from old shopping lists to pages from
damaged books, contain references to domestic life, which
we like to use. Any found material is further transformed
by mark-making (drawing, painting, printmaking and stitch
techniques), and marked pieces can then be exchanged and
used in each other's work during our workshop days.

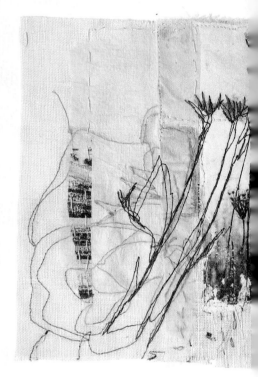

Right: *Lea Valley* and *High
Holborn Rooftops* (Cas Holmes
and Anne Kelly). Two small pieces
that reveal intricate stitching
and demonstrate different
handling of layers.

High Holborn 2   . A·Kelly '11

Stitch: an extension of mark-making

Anne's work is densely stitched and Cas's is open and painterly. Machine- and hand-stitching are used throughout our work, as a means to hold the textiles together as well as for embellishment and mark-making, and as a drawing tool. We often exchange pre-stitched pieces and fragments of older pieces to incorporate into works we develop for collaborative projects. Free-machine embroidery has emerged as an important component of our work, reinforcing our drawing and echoing our training as fine artists.

Left: *Domestic Mapping* (Anne Kelly). Detail showing stitched elements.

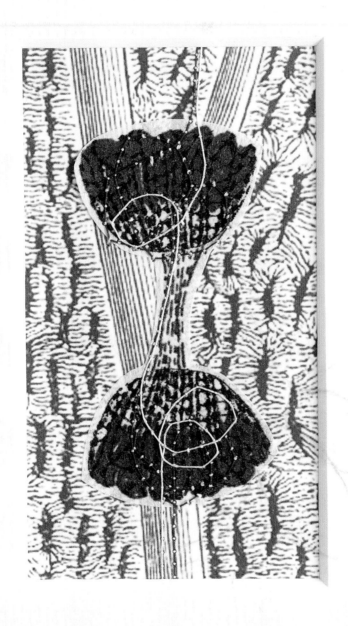

Above: This embroidered piece by Jenny Newson demonstrates a complex print, in which the stitch adds a more defined textured line to the surface.

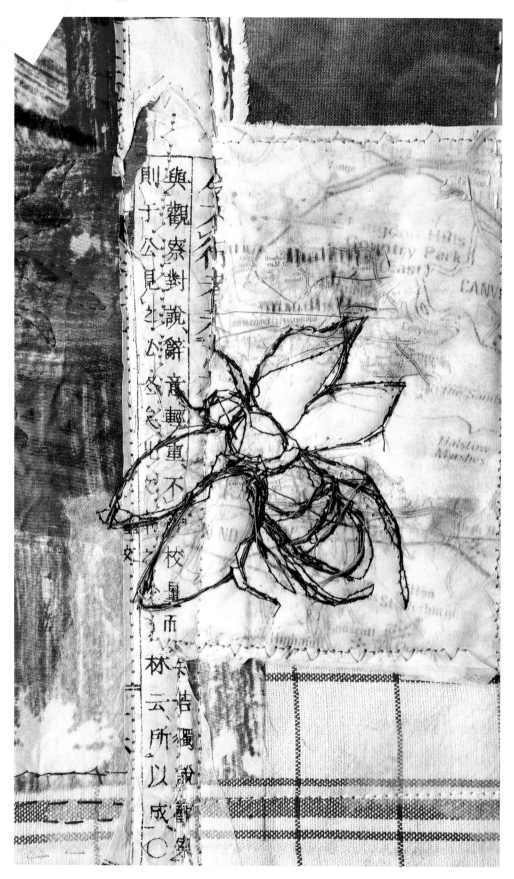

Left: *Domestic Mapping* (Cas Holmes). Bee detail showing stitched elements.

Right: *Domestic Mapping* (detail) (Cas Holmes [top] and Anne Kelly [bottom]). In this image we demonstrate different uses of print. The butterfly is overlaid with a print made from a stencil on its right-hand side. At the bottom, a strip of Indian print in red and white demonstrates the use of swapped found fabric. Anne also used vintage fabric sourced by herself.

Right and below: *Seed Bird Map* boxes for installation pieces (Top, Cas Holmes and bottom, Anne Kelly). In our collaborations, packaging and presentation is considered part of the design process. We usually start with similar component parts. In this case, seed packets and the illustrated text determined the width of the work. The final installation (see page 11) folds neatly into the packet wrapper. Our individuality is demonstrated in the boxes' shape, size and decoration.

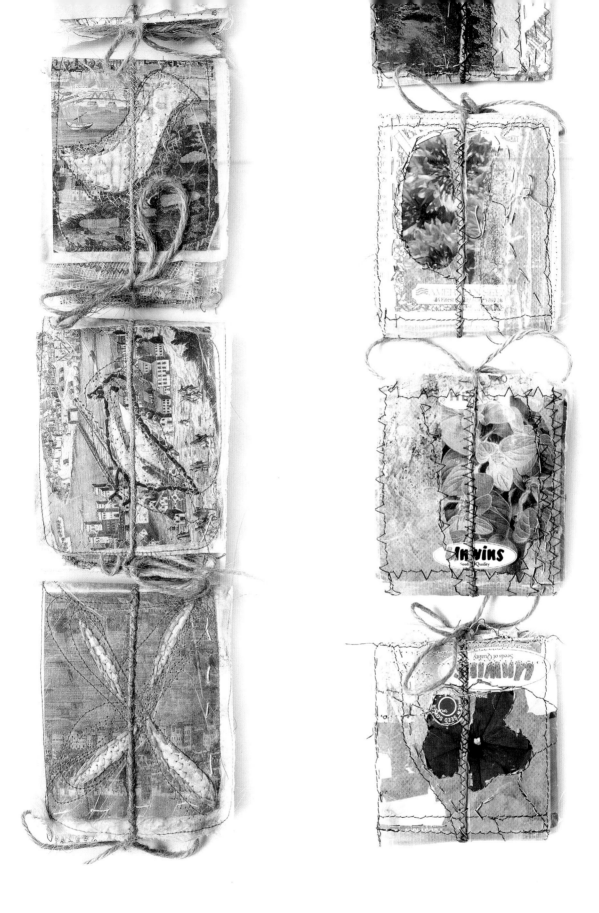

Above: *Seed Bird Map* (detail) (Anne Kelly
[left] and Cas Holmes [right]). This detail shows
the work in its outer wrapper, demonstrating
different handling of colours.

Starting points for themes and ideas

A good way to start working collaboratively is to exchange fabrics and the inspirations they provide. The materials you collect may well suggest the theme for a finished work. Florals may link with looking at a garden or nature; vintage fabrics and lace suggest something of historical interest, or the work could be tied to a simple colour theme. Where and how materials were collected could be tied into recollections of a journey or places visited together. These can then be shared and exchanged. For example, for our 'Cuttings' project, we decided to make reference to a regular railway journey between Maidstone and Tunbridge Wells that we both share.

When making a collection for a group project, consider the following:

- Collect fabrics and references that relate to a chosen theme (such as flora or a colour) that may work well for group exhibitions.

- Don't discount any paper or fabric remnant, as these can form useful elements of a larger piece and may add that 'finishing touch' to a future piece of work.

- Decide whether you wish to include some kind of uniformity or connected element, such as size, shape, colour or how you present the work.

- Each person can start off with a small collection of identical fabrics and papers, which can be used in their entirety or in each artist's work.

- Swap bags containing waste cut-outs and fragments from your own practice, or found items that may be of interest to the other person.

- Make observational drawings or paintings from a similar starting point.

Right: A mixture of found materials we exchanged and shared in preparation for *Cuttings*, a piece about our daily railway journeys.

Collage

The materials for our collages are drawn from our mutual collections. Collage brings together different elements and is a montage of various things – paper, fabric, rubbings, photographs and collected objects. When developing a piece, we consider how the collected elements relate to our themes. The materials collected could be a useful stimulus or starting point for a collage. There are many ways of using or approaching collage:

- Your collage may be colour-themed. Look at how combinations of colours may support your ideas in the materials you use. Staining or painting collected materials can also bring disparate elements together.

- You might choose a narrative approach, using items suggesting themes, such as a 'day in a garden'. You can also include words and verse to convey your ideas.

- Treat the collage like a research tool, incorporating images from magazines, your own photographs and other found resources to create a storyboard and references for future work.

- Collage can be used in combination with other media, such as paint, print, drawing media and stitch, to work up designs and ideas for future projects.

Print and Collage

We both use print and mark-making as part of the process of creating collage pieces, and often share resources to see where our ideas will lead. Even when starting with similar materials, we have found that our outcomes are always handled differently, in keeping with our personal style and approach. Our collages reflect the lines and marks of our drawing and the references and images we like using. Making samples, or small pieces, helps us to evolve our ideas and these samples are often incorporated into larger panels. As collage elements, the samples could work equally well in other textile pieces, such as cushion covers, items of clothing, quilts or bedcovers.

Opposite: *Cuttings* (Anne Kelly). This piece shows various found and printed images of crows, old maps, vintage fabric and transfers from old books.

Top right: Found elements laid out.
Right: Work in progress: starting to stitch the fabrics together.
Below: Our works in progress, shown side by side.

balance wheel
stop motion

Above: *Cuttings* (Cas Holmes). Sun-printed images, tea towel, tickets and maps. We made eight pieces in total, all the same width but in different lengths. The pieces all incorporate similar elements but have completely different colour palettes.

A stencilled collage

If you are new to collage, you might like to start with a stencilled work.

Materials

- Plain white or off-white fabric — an old piece of table linen, a tea towel or a pillowslip would provide a great background
- A piece of thin card or heavy cartridge paper (A4 size)
- Some acrylic or fabric paints and small sponges
- Pencil and thin felt-tipped pen
- A scalpel or scissors
- Assorted ribbons, lace scraps, old buttons, scraps of interesting fabric and paper
- Pictures of flora or fauna, preferably vintage ones
- Pins
- Sewing needles and threads, of different sizes and colours
- Perle cotton
- Sewing machine

Making the collage

1. Place a small collection of items in a pile for shared use.

2. Draw some floral shapes on to the cartridge or thin card with a pencil. Practise your drawings until you are happy with the shapes. Using the felt-tipped pen, go back over the simple shapes that you wish to cut out, ensuring that you leave sufficient space/tags between shapes so the stencil remains intact.

3. Print on to the scraps of fabric, using a brush or sponge and paints. Dab the paint on through the stencil; less is better than more! Leave the scraps to dry, which shouldn't take too long. Cutting out stencils with pinking shears or giving the shapes torn or 'raw' edges can also be effective.

4. Arrange cut pieces of found fabric, lace and ribbons on the base fabric in an interesting pattern. Use stronger colours to break up the background. Pin this arrangement and stitch it together, either by hand basting or with the machine. Finally you can add your stencilled image(s), either as whole pieces or in sections, stitching them firmly in place.

5. When you have stitched everything together, you can embellish the work with hand embroidery or even add some buttons. Your artwork can be stitched to backing fabric and used as a cushion cover or decorative insert. If so, you may need to consider how you will clean your work, depending on the materials used to make it.

Cut the stencil carefully, leaving a clearly defined shape.

Place the stencil on the fabric and dab on the paint with a brush or sponge to give a 'positive' print.

Do not waste anything — the cut-away sections of the stencil can be laid on cloth to give a 'negative' print.

ary these simple instructions to create a range of works based on other motifs, such as birds and their surroundings, leaves or insects. Small shapes of cloth with poems, writing or notes printed on them could suggest a story within the piece. Explore other methods of making marks, such as printing with rubber stamps to create patterns or words. You might make rubbings with fabric crayons from textured surfaces, such as a leaf or some lace, or use transfers of your own photographs and drawings. This can add additional interest and emphasis to areas of your fabric.

When working up a textile collage and combining elements with drawing and paint, you can use stitch or glue to anchor elements together initially. Our approach is similar in that we use layered fabrics and paper, but the specific way we each handle the processes differs in two key areas. Anne usually works with layers of fabric and some paper with stitch to provide a richly layered and strongly textured base 'fabric', to which additional elements, drawings and motifs are stitched and sometimes glued. Cas uses layers of paper and fabric pasted together. This initially changes the feel of the 'base fabric', providing a temporary hold when working on the machine or by hand, with elements being added or removed as they are worked. These steps broadly describe our base process, but as we work the pieces are constantly being reorganized, stitched and drawn into as they evolve.

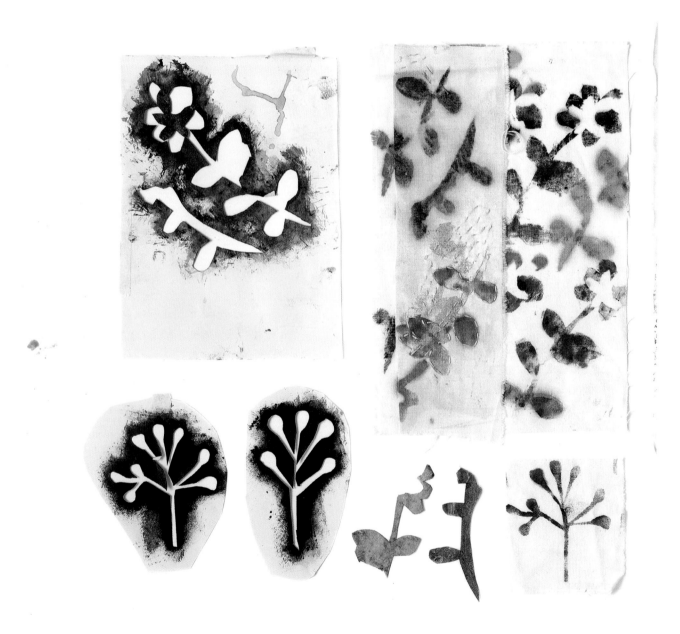

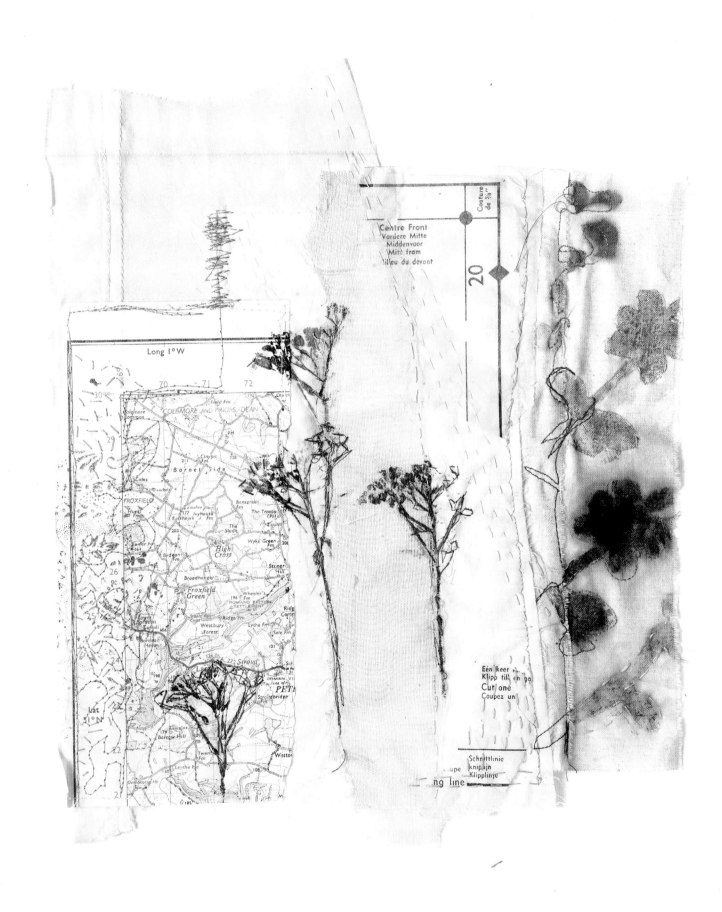

Left: Stencils, stencilled fabric and stitched floral images in progress.

Above: *Flora Map* (Cas Holmes). Stencils, collage, paper and stitch were used for this piece.

Transferring images

We use a number of methods to apply images, drawings and photographs to our work. We may draw directly on to the fabric, print as described on page 41, or print and transfer drawings or photos. Photographic transfer paper is widely available and images can be scanned or copied, which often works well with T-shirts or on tightly woven fabrics. The image is ironed on to the surface, fixing it to the fabric. We describe the basic process below. Other methods involve the use of transfer gels and media that you paint on the surface of the printed image, after which you lay the treated image on to the fabric for the transfer.

If using lettering, or where it is important for the image to remain the right way round, you will need to reverse your image first. Most photo-editing or word-processing programs on your computer will have a function for this. You can also use even the most basic photo-editing software to change the colour, scale, shapes and much more. We both use computer software in a more direct way, preferring to leave the image as we have created it, and much of the overlaying and transforming will be physical, as we work into our textiles with mark-making and stitch.

Iron-on transfers

There are many methods that you can use for transferring images. Here, we refer to iron-on processes that are are designed to work with inkjet, laser or photocopy images.

1. Print your image on to the transfer paper. Check with the manufacturer's directions for different types of paper first.

2. Pre-heat a non-steam iron or switch your steam setting off.

3. Place protective fabric on your ironing board/surface.

4. Iron the fabric to smooth out creases so it is ready to receive the print.

5. Place the printed paper on the fabric, image side down.

6. Press firmly with the iron, moving continuously for three or four minutes.

Check a corner to see if the image has adhered to the fabric and then peel off the paper backing to reveal the image.

Above: *Fly* (Anne Kelly).
24 x 24cm (9½ x 9½in). Black-and-white transfer images on an upcycled handkerchief, with a painted and overstitched insect.

Right: *Red Berries* (Cas Holmes). 110 x 48cm (43¼ x 19in). In this piece, the image from the photograph opposite was transferred and stitched. The crow was made from a black-and-white transfer image of a bird in a tree.

Stitch as a mark-making tool

Stitch can be used as a means of anchoring fabrics together or to make a mark. We often carry small pieces of fabric around for stitching while going about our daily lives. These small pieces can later be inserted into larger layered pieces. Our stitched marks are as different as one person's drawing is from another's. Below, we suggest some exercises that will help you to develop your mark-making in stitch.

- Make some simple line drawings of your subject (flora, patterns, still-life objects) and then machine stitch the drawings. If you are able to create continuous line drawings of your subject, you will find it easier to overstitch them by machine.

- Share stitches and create new approaches. A good shared project is to fold a piece of paper into different sections and pass it around the group, asking each person to make a textured mark or a quick sketch of related subject matter, before passing it on to the next person. Make a textile stitch sampler referencing these marks. As you look at and respond to the different marks, this helps to develop a more imaginative approach to your use of stitch.

- Look at examples of other types of stitching from your travels or holidays. Every country or culture has a history of stitch and embellishment, so collect images and samples. It's often worth visiting your local museum or gallery, as some have good collections of historical textiles. Books are also a good reference (Constance Howard's *Book of Stitches*, Batsford, 1979, is a classic that is always worth looking at).

A group workshop learning to use stitch can have an enjoyable session exploiting the tools used for making stitched marks. Think about the following:

- **What can you do with a regular machine stitch?** Explore different settings and investigate how you can vary the stitch. Most basic machines come with a few variations of utility and decorative stitches. Look at how you can use these. Vary the density and width of lines and overlay stitches. Make a grid and then let each person create line variations in their area, before passing the cloth to the next machine.

- **How can you make use of free machining or the darning foot?** Paper attached to the back of a fabric will give stability for experiments with an embroidery or darning foot. Exploit how the free motion of the needle gives you more flexibility to 'draw' across the surface of the material. As always, it is good practice to start with a line drawing as a basis for your image.

- **How do different materials respond?** Collect a variety of threads and surfaces to share for a hand-stitching session. Pass pieces around randomly, so that you work with cloth and thread you might not usually choose. Look at different needles, from darning needles to sailmaker's needles, and find out what sort of lines and marks you can make with the threads available. You can also pass a stitch sampler from person to person around the group.

When investigating marks for stitch consider all of the following:

- **Line** – straight/curved, broken, hard, soft

- **Texture** – creased fabric, broken lines, mix of thick/thin threads

- **Shapes** – circle, square, oblong, organic, mathematical patterns

- **Layers** – overlaying colours, paper, fabric, patterns, images

- **Colour** – use it for contrast, light against dark, and emphasis (it can be helpful to arrange threads into colour groups).

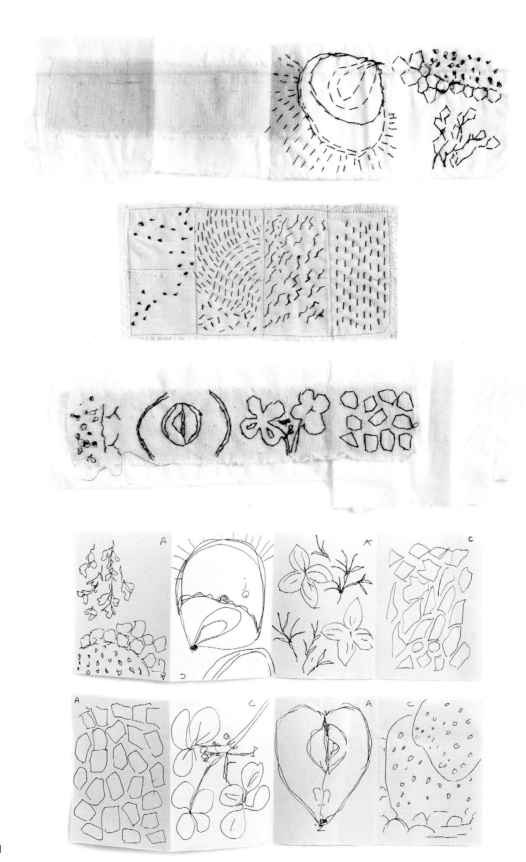

Opposite: A stitch workshop in progress.

Right: Stitched samples. The top two are by Cas Holmes and the middle one by Anne Kelly. At the bottom are line drawings exchanged between us and used as reference for the stitched samples.

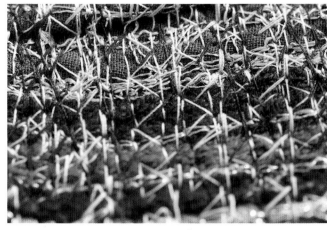

Above and right (detail): *Red Shoe* (Anne Kelly). An intensely worked stitched surface, showing found objects in an intimate still-life composition.

Above: *Winter Sun* (Cas Holmes). 110 x 48cm (43¼ x 19in).

Above right: *Spring Equinox* (Cas Holmes). 112 x 42cm
(44 x 16½in). The delicate 'drawing' is produced in stitch.

Connecting our work to others

Some of our approaches to exchanging materials form a useful base or starting point for community-based workshops. When exhibiting at the Town and Country Gallery at the Trinity Theatre, Tunbridge Wells, we worked with local students, supplying fabrics and papers and using a connection with our work 'Seed Bird Map' to help them create folding sketchbooks. Prior to the workshop, we discussed how we would organize the session, what tools and materials we would need and how we could balance our approach with the needs of the students and the curriculum.

We began the session with an introductory look around the exhibition and talked to the group, explaining our themes and inspiration. Relating ideas around mapping, we discussed how they might make a record of what they saw around them. The students had a variety of learning disabilities and were accompanied by the appropriate teaching staff, who assisted with the interpretation and gave additional support where it was necessary.

We split the group in two and started with a drawing exercise. Students identified images from the work around them to use as a starting point for their own drawing. We constantly made reference to the importance of drawing in our work as a means to record and interpret what we see.

Using some of the materials the students brought with them, combined with the selection that we supplied as part of the overall theme of the workshop, the students created folding collaged sketchbooks. These were completed back at school and formed a relevant part of their school curriculum work.

The students' experiences from the workshop were recorded in photos and comments, and this, together with their finished collaged books, will form part of their AQA GCSE or Entry Level coursework, contributing to assessment objectives in both. Meeting artists and experiencing art first hand is a valuable learning experience for our students; it validates their study of the subject and provides insight into the range of artistic possibilities and opportunities open to them.

Right: Students making books inspired by the work around them in a gallery.

Below: Diagram for a simple folding book.

Jo Week, Art Teacher,
Oakley School

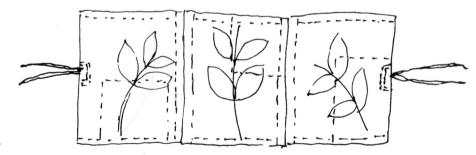

Left : *Folding Slate Book* (Cas Holmes). This triangular folded book is made with Japanese paper and has a cover made from slate left over from tiling a bathroom.

Right : *Bird Book* (Anne Kelly). The cover of the book features a simple stencilled bird on vintage furnishing fabric.

On reflection

Our creative collaboration has never remained static. Email remains one of the most important tools for expressing our thoughts, feelings and ideas. When we started working together, we freely exchanged materials and ideas as we discovered and shared experiences and working methods, giving little time for reflection. Our first exhibitions gave us an opportunity to see the work together, reflect on progress and become more aware of our individual approaches within project themes. We have always recognized that our work reflects different approaches to shared or common themes. Through continued assessment, we have retained our individuality within the collaborative process, as a part of our own creative practice. As we move forward, we have our own ideas (and egos) to contend with, as well as the demands and needs of other projects. We have learnt to face up to any difficulties or anxieties we have about our work and have been prepared to challenge as well as support each other. Working together has enabled us to arrive at the current position of Resonant Textiles. We still meet, share materials and exchange ideas, seeking the benefits of the 'resonant' within our work through collaboration, while retaining and respecting our personal creative languages. The long-term benefits and rewards of sharing our work with each other and the public make it all worthwhile.

Right: *Parks in Common* (detail).
Left: *Wellington Rocks* (Anne
Kelly). Right: *Shared Paths* (Cas
Holmes). The printed bird images
of Anne's piece contrast with the
layers of lace and stitched prints
in Cas's work.

Left: *Wellington Rocks* (Anne
Kelly). Cover for folding book.

Below: *Shared Paths* (Cas
Holmes). Cover for book.

2 Exhibitions, Museums and Artists' Collaborations

Joint exhibitions and projects are a great source of inspiration for artists and makers. The collaborative process of putting on a joint show always opens up new, often unexpected avenues for future work and provides participants with a forum in which to exchange ideas and explore new interests. In this section, we look at the advantages of belonging to a group and the practicalities of organizing an exhibition, as well as giving examples of other types of collaborative exhibition and project.

Joining or organising a group

At certain stages in your career, belonging to a group or organization will fulfil various functions. The type of group you belong to will rarely remain static and, when joining a group, it is worth looking online at examples of members' work and the specifics of that organization to find out if they appeal to your current needs. Some organizations have open membership, including many online groups of people who share similar interests. National and international organizations, such as the Quilters' Guild and the Embroiderers' Guild in the UK, the Surface Design Association in the USA and the European Textile Network, are a rich source of information on textiles and stitch. They provide opportunities to meet and create together, as well as information on activities, from local to international level. Other groups, such as the 62 Group and Quilt 25, have a selected membership. Both of these latter organizations exhibit contemporary textiles internationally.

Your choice of group may depend on its having an accessible location, providing opportunities for you to meet with other members on a more informal basis. Acting as a mutual support network, smaller groups (perhaps even as small as just two members) allow for an exchange and sharing of skills that could lead to exhibiting possibilities.

We, the writers, work together as a means to share and review our work and assess what we can learn from it. Our work is complementary in subject matter and scale and often extends to working with other people and organizations. As part of our ongoing collaboration, we reflect on and critique the process and develop new approaches, which have led to further opportunities, including exhibitions.

Previous pages: *Domestic Mapping: Australian Bee* (detail) (Cas Holmes). Mixed media on tea towel. **Above:** *Norfolk Weeds* (top, Anne Kelly and bottom, Cas Holmes).

Working towards an exhibition

Artists and makers often find themselves organizing their own exhibitions and events. Suitable spaces in arts centres, colleges, workplaces, libraries, schools and even shops can provide an alternative to the more formal gallery. There is a market for moderately sized and reasonably priced exhibitions that appeal to different audiences and tastes, and artists' groups can make a valuable contribution to their communities by showing at local venues. The normal way for artists to secure an exhibition is to send details, a CV and images of work to those galleries and exhibitions which accept applications. Larger, established (and often subsidized) galleries, as a general rule, rarely welcome applications, and artists are either invited to exhibit or participate in a juried selection process.

Be realistic

Organizing an exhibition of any type is a major undertaking and can be very costly in time and money, so you need to be prepared for this. Modest-sized exhibitions can be organized with limited funds; on the other hand, larger projects are more likely to attract grant aid. It is essential at the outset to decide carefully on the size and content of the exhibition. Two moderately sized venues, Maidstone Library Gallery and Farnham Maltings Gallery, where we toured 'Natural Histories', were ideal in terms of size and in their relationship to their localities and the communities they support.

Think ahead

Most galleries are booked up between six and 24 months ahead, or longer for major exhibitions. You should allow at least 12 months between the booking and the showing date: adding your time in creating pieces and working on the concept for the show, this amounts to a total of at least 18 months' preparation. We worked on 'Natural Histories' for two years, while also seeking venues. Arrangements rarely fell neatly into place and the project took considerable administration! The first rule is to plan well ahead, as this can reduce time and costs.

Finding suitable venues

It is essential to draw up a shortlist of suitable exhibition spaces to which to send your details. Check that you are not sending them to venues that are too small, don't show the medium in which you work, or have a programming policy that may exclude you (for example, some venues are only open to local artists or sculpture-based exhibitions). Read the exhibition listings in art/craft/photography magazines or online to find out what kind of exhibitions individual galleries are showing.

Funding

Whether you are an individual or work in collaboration or within an artists' group, it is rare to be offered a grant to cover the cost of the exhibition. Much of our exhibition work we have financed and administrated ourselves, yet it is sometimes possible to raise sponsorship or funding, often from apparently unlikely sources. For our 'Domestic Mapping' exhibition at Trinity Arts Centre in Tunbridge Wells, we ran a day of workshops with the local community in exchange for the gallery-hire fee.

Budgeting

Draw up a list of the things you need to consider when planning an exhibition. Many of the costs may be absorbed or taken on by the host gallery. It is useful to go through a costing exercise, especially if you are applying for funding. Now that exhibitions are often publicized through social media and artists' websites, mailing invites is often unnecessary. You do, however, need to cover photographs, telephone calls, items for promotion and publicity, equipment for hanging, insurance, transport and accommodation. These expenses could be offset by sales and fees for workshops.

Selling your exhibition to galleries

The information you send should be concise and should give a clear description of your work and the purpose of the exhibition. Initially, we send an email or letter of introduction along with a proposal to a specific, named person, if we can. We also include our CVs (for a group exhibition, we send a brief résumé, rather than a full CV for each group member) and a few images of work, as a taster. It is useful to keep a checklist of the galleries to which you have sent information.

The introduction letter or email should outline the proposed exhibition, giving contact details and any further information that is available via links to websites. It should contain some, if not all, of the following:

- A brief description of the work and purpose or rationale behind the exhibition.

- The number and size of the proposed exhibits.

- Availability – give the dates when the exhibition is to be made available.

Following up

Programme selection is handled differently by each gallery or venue. Some exhibitions may be selected through a collective selection process or a panel. In this case, you need to check deadlines and, where relevant, follow up to the same named person to whom you first sent the application. If you get to the next stage, you will need to negotiate and discuss the following items:

- Transport – if special arrangements are needed, discuss who will be responsible for transporting the exhibition and what kind/size of transport is required.

- Packaging – how are the works to be packaged? Good labelling is important, as you may not be unpacking and packing the work yourself.

- Insurance – who is responsible for arranging and paying for insurance? In addition to insuring the work, you will also need Public Liability Insurance, as a group or individual. (This insures you in case an accident occurs causing damage or injury to a third partydue to the exhibition.)

- Invitations and cards, catalogues or information leaflet: is the venue going to include these within their costs for the exhibition? If so, how many of each will they pay for and who is responsible for arranging this?

- Press information – when is this needed by and who deals with this?

- Are there any other requirements (showcases, plinths) that the gallery should supply, or any limitations on showing the work (lighting, humidity, security control)?

- Extra activities – are you offering any extra exhibition activities (such as talks or workshops)?

It is very unlikely that you will have all this information established at this stage, but give as much detail as you can and clearly describe the information as 'provisional'. These details are best negotiated on a one-to-one basis over the telephone after the information has been received by the gallery or galleries.

Left: *Cuttings* (Cas Holmes and Anne Kelly) on show at ReCall Studios, Tunbridge Wells. The pieces float against the dark blue walls of the dance studio where the work was exhibited.

Below: *Whole Moth Tablecloth* (Anne Kelly, foreground) and *Imperfect Plant* (Cas Holmes, background), exhibited at Farnham Maltings, part of our first collaborative exhibition, 'Natural Histories'.

Preparing for the exhibition

Working towards your exhibition requires everyone to meet the deadlines. You will need to consider such matters as promotion across the venues, how you will get the work to the exhibition space at the right time and how you will relate your work to the complexities of the space through appropriate hanging. Any communication with galleries or venues to finalize all arrangements should be followed up with an email or phone call, where necessary.

Printing/publicity

Good-quality images are important, whether you are representing your work online, or in a catalogue or poster, or giving information to the press. We look at the design considerations (format and scale), but prefer to use the same image, where possible, across all areas of promotion. Using several communication media for presentation helps you to cast the net wider and reach a larger audience. Here are a few tips:

- Avoid using 'artspeak': use language that will attract a wider audience.

- Promotion material must contain, in clear lettering, the title, date, gallery, address, opening hours and accessibility (and if you have had support towards the exhibition costs, don't forget to acknowledge this!).

- You will need posters for each venue where you're exhibiting and, for general promotional purposes, also allow some for the exhibiting artists to distribute locally to libraries and public spaces, as well as to friends, family and colleagues.

- Make postcards, the backs of which can be printed for a variety of purposes (invitation card; biography or artist's statement; list of exhibits). If the exhibition features a number of artists, a card for each can be collected together into a plastic wallet or envelope and sold as a catalogue. The cards can also be used individually.

- Is a catalogue necessary, and what function would it serve? Online catalogues or websites are a greener method of showcasing your work.

- Press pack – ensure that you contact local press and any further media contacts you may have, as this can be a great way of raising awareness of your work and exhibition. This can also provide a forum for reviews of your work.

Left: *High Holborn Rooftops* (detail) (Anne Kelly). Richly worked and layered surface, showing the 'webbing' effect of concentrated machine stitch.

Information and labels for exhibits

Find out if you must supply these yourself. Labelling for each exhibit should be legible from at least 100cm (40in) away, mounted on card or laminated and blue-tacked to the wall behind, and should give the name of the artist, title (and catalogue number) and selling price. An information leaflet or a panel on the wall enables visitors to understand and appreciate the work. This can be either a simply typed and photocopied A4 sheet or a commercially produced brochure, depending on your budget.

Hanging and launch

Agree a time and date and find out beforehand the nature of the surfaces you will be working on. What additional help and equipment (staff, steps, tools and so on) may be available? Is there a private view and, if so, who pays for it? Is the space accessible for wheelchair users? If not, you must note this and apologize in your publicity.

It is always a good idea to review and reflect on your exhibition. A comments book allows for informal feedback and people can leave contact details. Invite a colleague or visitor to write about the exhibition and suggest which publications may be happy to take a review. The following was written for *Embroidery* magazine. A shorter, punchier comment may be more appropriate for a local newspaper:

Nature is everywhere apparent in both artists' work: finely machine-stitched drawings of birds, insects and elegant tall-stemmed plants, wild and cultivated, as well as pages from plant and bird books embedded in stitchery. The long panels of their 'Garden Path' series also combine, in a painterly way, in their verticality and colour – soft lilacs and greens echo each other from one long panel to the next. This orderliness, gentleness of colour and delicacy of drawing runs through the whole show.

Anne's individual pieces are mostly framed, and even within the space are often bordered and centred, firmly holding together the disparate elements of collage, such as straw hats, as do also her webs of machine stitching, which, as in 'Tudeley', give a layered effect. This webbing is particularly successful in her three small panels, 'High Holborn Rooftops', where green leaves of a spring evening sharply contrast with the blues and slate greys, and gold – as of a lighted shop window – gleams through the dense web.

In Cas' case, the layers are produced through areas of found fabrics and dyes, as well as more open quilting and painted text. Her composition is achieved through the internal organization of verticals and horizontals, leaving a feeling of openness. Her pieces 'Red Madder' and 'Bluebell', for example, seem to float off the wall, retaining the glow as well as the formality of a Rothko.

Janet Sturge, *Embroidery* magazine, October 2010

Right: *Red Madder* (Cas Holmes). 100 x 100cm (3 x 3ft). Old tablecloths, furnishing fabrics and napkins layered with printed plants and stitched plant drawings.

Practical suggestions for hanging textiles

Do not underestimate just how long it can take to hang an exhibition. Having a basic but well-organized tool kit is essential. Fishing line, needles and strong thread are useful for hanging and securing work, and you will need clean fabric or plastic dustsheets on which to lay work.

When we decide to produce a joint piece for installation or exhibition together, we firstly take into consideration the space and/or criteria of the show for which it is intended. Although we work independently on pieces, we may discuss certain common elements beforehand, such as:

- Colour schemes, format, scale

- Starting points

- Types of found materials

- Suitability of the space in which we are hanging the work

- Methods of hanging to be used.

During the production of pieces, we get together to compare notes and photograph the works at different stages, both for our records and to act as an *aide-mémoire*. A rough plan is drawn up after a visit to the space, and we always take more work than we need and choose from this collection. Collaborative work is accessible and sometimes free-hanging, so must be displayed in a robust way. It is generally a good idea to monitor your exhibition at regular intervals to ensure there is no damage or unexpected change to your work. Our work is often designed so that visitors can interact with the pieces. This is apparent in the way they are exhibited, as in 'Seed Bird Map'.

In one corner, hung floor to ceiling there was a collaborative series of hanging sketchbooks using fabric, paper and stitch. They were absolutely delightful. Unsophisticated and free, they were an intriguing record of place, which felt as though they had been completed 'en plein air'. The exhibition is greatly strengthened by the two artists' explanations of how they have developed their ideas and some of the techniques they have used.

Extract from Brenda Parsons' review for
Embroidery magazine, March 2010

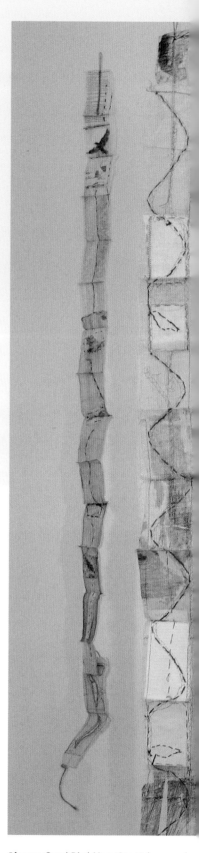

Above: *Seed Bird Map* (Cas Holmes and Anne Kelly). Installation at Trinity Town and Country Gallery, Tunbridge Wells.

Framing and presenting work

We both use a variety of methods to hang or display our work, whether free-hanging or framed. Presentation needs to be considered as you make the piece.

- Large pieces can look dramatic unframed. An additional backing can be sewn to the work to help protect the piece. Onto this, sew a pocket (8–10cm/3–4in deep) to the top, along the back of a work. This provides a useful alternative to Velcro as a hanging device. You can add another pocket at the bottom to carry a batten to add weight to the hanging.

- Smaller works can be stretched over a canvas frame and stitched into position. Always make the piece larger than the frame, to give you enough material to wrap round to the back and stitch.

- More fragile or less 'stable' work is best protected in a frame. You can buy off-the-peg frames for smaller pieces. Stitching work on to good-quality watercolour paper before framing is a simple method that works well.

- Heavily textured pieces may need to be mounted and placed in a deeper box frame. These can be custom-made to your specifications by a good framing specialist, who will be happy to advise on different approaches to presenting your work. Whatever method you use for framing, it should enhance the work and, where possible, be reversible.

- Often, the work and environment will dictate how the piece is made and might be part of the construction of the piece. 'Seed Bird Map' used a simple thread running through the piece, and was hung using fishing wire.

Left, top: *British Birds: Great Tit* (Cas Holmes). Images taken from an old Ladybird book and old maps, layered and stitched on to canvas with paint and dye. Detail shown above right.

Left, bottom: *Small Embroidered Bird* (Anne Kelly). Stitched and painted bird on a background of vintage lace stretched over a canvas frame.

SEOS: the domestic space

About five years ago, we began taking part in an open studio programme, South East Open Studios (SEOS), with a diverse group of local artists. The programme included work in textiles, print, watercolour, paper-cuts and glass. The experience has had a great impact on our own work and, as participants in these events, we have had to take on board the additional considerations of organizing a group event in an open studio, which may not just be a workspace, but may also be your home.

South East Open Studios was established to help individual makers work together when showing their work. We often invite people to see our work, by appointment, in our home studios. Organizing a group of artists to exhibit throughout a month (in this case, June) in a suitable venue can be advantageous to participants, as it shares out the work and responsibility. It also provides visitors with an opportunity to meet artists in their workspace or studio, in a more relaxed domestic setting.

The lower floor and garden of Anne's three-storey Victorian house is an ideal exhibition space for SEOS. The house is within easy walking distance of a rail link, and the presence of other open studios in the vicinity made it the obvious candidate. The kitchen, living room and a garden outhouse provide three distinct settings for the artists' work. In the garden outhouse, 'The Shed', we display pieces with a

thematic or visual relationship to plants and natural scenery. The natural space complements these qualities in our work. In the house, we especially want visitors to see that artwork can resonate with elements of the domestic and familiar. In turn, this provides an approachable and welcoming environment for the visitor. Visitors have returned to our South East Open Studio exhibition in Kent yearly, as they identify the space and artwork as memorable.

Things to consider

When using your domestic space or studio as an exhibition venue, as opposed to exhibiting in a gallery, there are some additional things to consider:

- Have you got the right space (walls, fittings and so on) for displaying/presenting your work in the home?

Left: Visitors looking at *Corn Field* (Cas Holmes, right) and *Satchels* (Anne Kelly, left).

Opposite, top: *Norfolk Weeds* (detail) (Left, Anne Kelly and right, Cas Holmes). This installation was hung with a stained-glass panel by Gill Newson, creating a series of views through to the foliage outside the window.

Opposite, bottom left: *The Eye* (Anne Kelly).

Opposite, bottom right: Jenny Newson's work displayed on a shelf.

- How will you watch over/guard your show?

- As with any public event, what about access? It is helpful to point out any slippery paving, uneven surfaces and so on.

- Have good signposting. SEOS includes brochures and signage as part of the artist's pack.

We have tried to unite artists who share the theme of using the natural world as their inspiration. This adds coherence and stability to the exhibition. It also provides a range of work for visitors to look at, depending on their interests. The use of existing architectural features and furniture to display framed, free-standing and 3-D work enables visitors to visualize the work in their own home setting more easily.

When deciding which works to hang together, we lay out the pieces and select materials, textures and colours that work well together. When hanging the works, we allow spaces for labels and ensure that, although works may be close together, there is enough breathing space.

The South East Open Studios environment has been productive and encouraging for all the artists involved in our exhibitions. The feedback and educational element of the shows have lent a gravitas to the whole event and ensured that it continues to evolve and increase in popularity.

Other exhibition collaborations

There are all sorts of possible connections that could be used as the basis for an exhibition, from a shared medium or subject to a colour theme or even a specified format. Where membership is spread over a broad geographical area, good communication is important. Transportation of the work also needs to be factored in to the design of the exhibition.

The Knitting and Stitching Shows at Harrogate, London and Dublin and the Festival of Quilts at the NEC in Birmingham are a main focus for textile practitioners in the UK and abroad, and provide great forums for exchange. We have both participated in these events for many years as observers, educationalists and artists. Taking part can lead to many offshoots, such as joint touring exhibitions, sales and workshops, and can increase your profile.

A selected exhibition: Freiheit. Liberté. Freedom. (Anne Kelly)

My collaboration with Gudrun Heinz, a German textile artist, and the exhibition 'Freiheit. Liberté. Freedom.' came about through a competition entry that was advertised on several textile and fibre-art sites. I submitted two pieces based on the theme, one of which was selected from over two hundred entries from several European countries. Gudrun has organized three other challenges and considers arranging the work to be like piecing together a large patchwork quilt, matching colours and themes. The entries were each stitched to a piece of backing fabric, all of the same size, enabling the work to be transported and organized for exhibition display more easily.

The exhibition opened at the Festival of Quilts in Birmingham in August 2011 and toured to Moscow, Prague and Einbeck in Germany. The CD-ROM that accompanied the exhibition on its tour was a useful alternative to a catalogue. This exhibition was eclectic in feel, demonstrating a wide variety of textile media and interpretations of a theme in a good range of small-sized projects.

Right: *Chinese Liberty* (Anne Kelly). Layered embroidery with silk and paper elements.

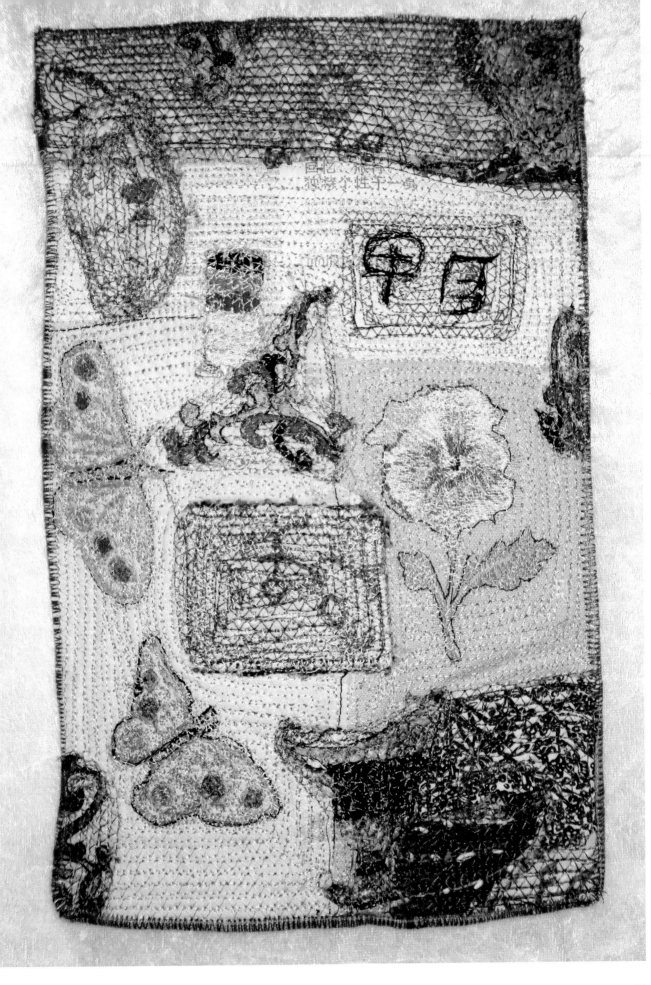

Left: Suggested layouts for wall display and panel arrangements.

Above: The *Freiheit. Liberté. Freedom* touring exhibition at the Festival of Quilts, UK, 2011.

Gudrun describes the selection process as follows:

The overall design of the final display was set from the beginning, determined by transportation and display requirements, (e.g. dimension of the whole display, size of the carrier panels and how to fold them for transportation, etc.)

The criteria for selecting the pieces of work and how to display them included:

- Considering the combinations of colour and elements of design.

- Finding the right position for each of the pieces within the display.

- Finally, developing an appealing balance of work.

At first a jury of three sorted all the entered pieces into groups for their inclusion – criteria for selection were message, creativity and interpretation, as well as good craftsmanship.

Pieces were sorted by colour. It was noticed that, though entered by completely different artists, there were some preferred colour combinations, like shades of yellows in combination with shades of violets and pinks. Other colours used were more sedate, and we looked at adding contrasting colour or grids in various styles to give the group a structure and lead the viewer's eyes over each panel. The final 18 panels were connected by their colours and the positioning of the work, lending a pleasing rhythm to the exhibited pieces.

Gudrun Heinz, Coordinator

International Year of Forests 2011 (Cas Holmes)

The United Nations General Assembly declared 2011 as the International Year of Forests to raise awareness of sustainable management, conservation and development of all types of forest. The Forestry Research Institute at Baden-Wuerttemberg, Freiburg, as part of a global commemoration, invited 14 artists from Europe to exhibit work. Hanging space determined the size of the work (width 45cm x length 150cm/18 x 60in), which also allowed for smaller parcels to be rolled and posted to the organiser, Monika Schiwy of Quilt Star, thus keeping down expense.

With a focus on the local woodland spaces at Mote Park, where I live in Kent, I explored the role trees play in the urban environment, as well as stressing the importance of biodiversity within our varied woodland landscape. There is a constant challenge for space between the needs of people and the needs of the woodland. The park has been re-landscaped and improved with new pathways and hard-surface promenade areas, older trees being removed as part of this process of improvement. 'Woodland Floor', one of three related pieces, explores the rich woodland and includes fabric which had been buried in the park. Sun-printed images of ground-cutting tools, reflecting the groundwork undertaken as part of the building programme, were overstitched with machine drawings of plant forms.

Das Buch vom Wald (Picture Book of the Forest), by Helga Widmann, is composed of six panels made of antique woven linen from a flea market. The fabric was whitened with gesso and then painted with acrylics, to which coloured transfers were added.

The text is from an antiquarian book (110 years old) for teachers of young children, which has several chapters about the forest. I took part of the text of the book and wrote it by hand on organza because I wanted it to integrate well in the piece.

Helga Widmann

Left: *Picture Book of the Forest* (Helga Widmann).

Right: *Woodland Floor* (Cas Holmes). 180 x 40cm (6 x 1¼ft). This work features a sunprint of ground-cutting tools at the top-left corner. A detail from the work is shown on the right.

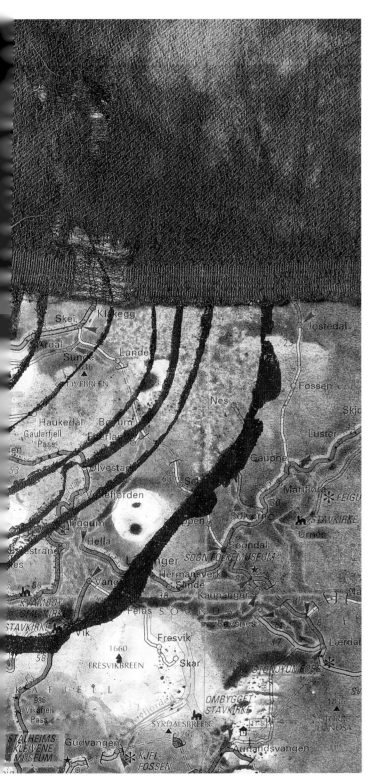

Els Van Baarle creates her own art fabrics on a commercial basis. These are often used by other quilt artists, including Cherllyn Martin, with whom she regularly collaborates in exhibitions. Her beautiful layered pieces combine wax resist and silk-screened dyed cotton and wool fabric with paper and stitch. She builds up her surfaces, layering wax–dye–wax–dye–wax–dye to achieve a great depth of colour. She uses traditional Indonesian tools – *tjanting* (wax drawing tools) and *tjap* (copper stamps) – as part of the process to make a contemporary, non-traditional fabric.

My work is always based on the past, fragments, old buildings, the wear and tear of time. Time is an important element. I did not want to make the trees in a pictorial way. Usually, nature, like trees, plants, is not my source of inspiration. To make a connection between TIME and TREE I decided to emphasize the lines that show the age of the tree.

The exploration of fabric collage gives freedom in the design process of Monika Schiwy's work. Transparent and non-transparent fabrics are layered and integrated with paper, printing and fabric-transfer methods on to a batting base. A top layer of thin chiffon scarf is worked with quilt and stitch techniques. This also prevents the textile surface from fraying.

I am interested in different things: nature, people and their paths of life, and their relations to each other. I like the graphic aspects of images, writing and text fragments – which, when altered, change the context and are 'alienated' from their origins.

Above: *Trees* (detail) (Els van Baarle).

Right: *Käfergeschichte 3* (Monika Schiwy).

Urban-Nature, Festival of Quilts and the Knitting and Stitching Show (Cas Holmes)

Working in preparation for Urban-Nature at the Festival of Quilts in Birmingham and the Knitting and Stitching Show at Alexandra Palace in London involved two years of experimenting with new approaches for my ideas as well as the complex planning needed for the space. Many of the materials used in the work came out of informal collaborations as part of my daily life, asking the people I met on a day-to-day basis if they would contribute old textiles, tablecloths, handkerchiefs and curtains to work with. Family and friends also sent images of plants from their locality. These included a series of wildflowers growing along the edges of the Lea Valley, the site heavily developed as part of the Olympic Park.

Careful planning of the gallery required mock-ups and plans to ensure exhibits fitted in with the template of the floor space allocated to each exhibitor. Everything required a great attention to detail and a number of conversations with colleagues and the team at Twisted Thread. Each exhibit had to be numbered to ensure it arrived at the right space, and setting up was undertaken with military precision by the event organizers. Although it is complex, collaboration with other exhibitors and trade stalls in major festival events provides a forum for interaction and presents opportunities to reach a varied audience of people who might not attend more formal gallery settings. Shared practice was demonstrated in the inclusion of 'Cuttings' (with Anne), and an ongoing stitched collaborative piece, 'Tea-Flora-Tales', composed of small pages from an old embroidery book. Visitors spent some time stitching flower patterns and teabags to their own pages, which were added to this 'daisy chain' piece. Some of the pieces were taken away to be finished and then later sent back to me by post.

Above: *Cuttings* (Anne Kelly [left] and Cas Holmes [right]), on location at the Knitting and Stitching Show, London, 2012.

Far right: *Tea-Flora-Tales* (Cas Holmes). Sample strip of a collaborative piece made by the Chelmsford branch of the Embroidery Guild.
Right: Materials collected for *Tea-Flora-Tales*.

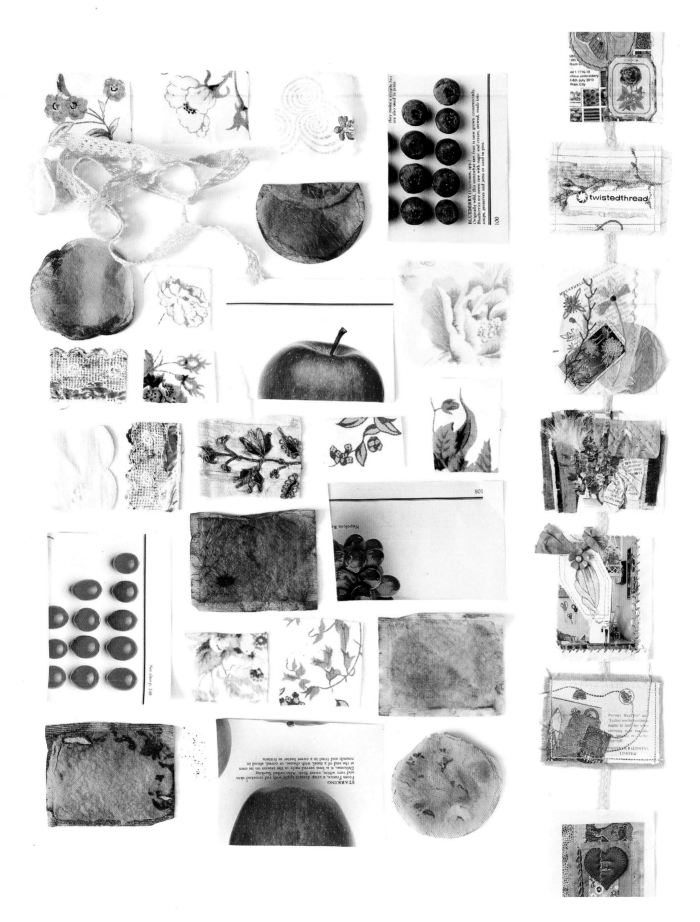

Above: *Wayside Grasses* (detail) (Cas Holmes). This installation piece varied from venue to venue and incorporated domestic fabrics donated by students from my local adult education centre.

Left: Cas Holmes installing *Wayside Grasses*.

Right: General shot of *Tea-Flora-Tales* at the Urban-Nature exhibition.

Ongoing collaboration as part of an exhibition or event

Demonstrating or involving people in some work can be a useful way to engage people with the process. For 'Tea-Flora-Tales', I found the following guidelines useful, and they would apply to any similar project.

- Keep the collaboration simple in a public space – ideally, the project should be something that can be done on the lap or without needing much in the way of additional resources. I stored all the necessary materials in two plastic food containers.

- Consider how the separate pieces may come together. The book pages determined the nature of this piece. Modular or folding forms work well, as these can be added to as they progress.

- Find a theme or image relevant to the exhibition or event. In this case, our theme was determined by the subject: protection of wildflowers on our verges.

- Make a small sample to demonstrate a possible approach, but be open to individuals making their own interpretation.

- Have some materials prepared and 'ready to go'. Pages pre-cut to size, teabags and a selection of fabrics and threads were available in this case.

- Be clear about the outcome. Will people be able to take the sample away if they wish, or is it to be added to an ongoing piece?

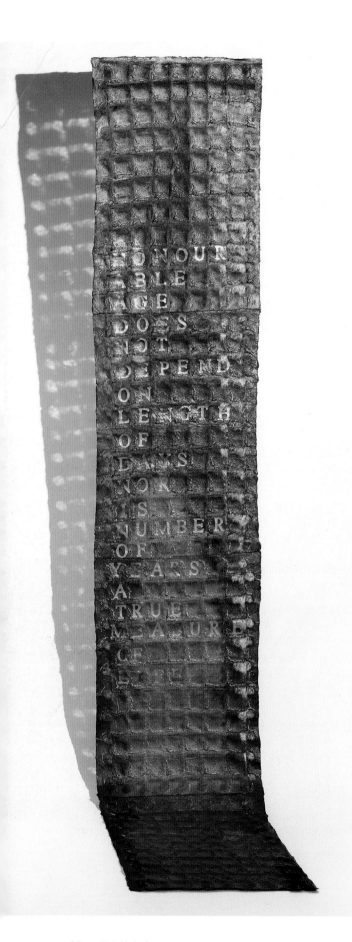

Quilt Art

Quilt Art, formed in 1985, is the oldest group of its kind in Europe. Together, its members work to increase recognition of the quilt as an art form. With over twenty members from the UK, Ireland, mainland Europe and the United States, collaborating across such a wide geographical area can pose difficulties, but the members are in constant touch via a Yahoo group site and try to attend at least two of the four meetings a year. Every two or three years, the group holds a major touring exhibition, accompanied by a self-published book.

There is no hierarchy within Quilt Art and each member is expected to contribute to the considerable workload of liaising with exhibition venues, dealing with publicity and selling books. A selection process ensures that members have an original artistic voice, high technical standards and a firm commitment to the group. All the members value the international friendships, artistic support and lively debates that come with belonging to Quilt Art.

Sara Impey, www.quiltart.eu

For the group's 25th anniversary celebrations, 'A Slice of Quilt Art', which opened at the Festival of Quilts in 2010, space was limited, so size restrictions were a determining factor as to the nature of the work on show. In most exhibitions, the artists are free to express themselves, but for some time the group had been informally discussing approaches to creating three-dimensional work and different methods of display. This exhibition offered an opportunity to put those ideas into practice, creating smaller works that extend the boundaries of quilting methods in design and approach. It was generally felt that this challenge led to one of the group's most cohesive and visually satisfying exhibitions.

It is clear that the success of any collaborative exhibition relies on good communication and networking and that participants must be prepared to fulfil certain roles. Artists local to the venue for a group exhibition may take on the main liaison and installation responsibilities, while other roles, such as administration, press and producing catalogues, are shared amongst the group.

Left: *Honourable Age* (Cherilyn Martin, 2009). 55 x 310cm (22 x 122in).

Presentation and transport of the work needs to be factored into the overall design of the exhibition. Often, simple formats can help this. In her Freedom exhibition (see page 70) Gudrun Heinz mounted the work on to panels according to theme. Restricting size and experimenting with hanging methods is another option and can contribute to a more cohesive display.

Exploring themes of commemoration, Cherilyn Martin, a British artist living in the Netherlands, created a poignant layered paper piece, *Honourable Age*, in response to the war in Iraq:

This piece was made in response to the Basra Memorial Wall, which was erected in Iraq and later returned and rebuilt in the U.K. I choose to work with paper to emphasize the fact that lives can be torn and shattered by war; the transparency of the paper emphasizes the fragility of life. The 179 red hand stitches on the work represent the 179 lives lost. The text 'Honourable Age' which is cited on the memorial wall is taken from the Book of Wisdom 4:8 in the Bible.

Right: *Four Slices* (Inge Hueber, 2009). Four pieces, each 14 x 275cm (5½ x 108in).

In contrast to Cherilyn Martin's commemorative work, founder member of the group Inge Hueber's piece, *Four Slices*, is a playful creation, composed of bright squares of colour pieced with one layer of home-dyed cotton and transparent cotton organza. This can be presented in different ways – hanging from the ceiling or rolled up in four rolls.

Several members opted for a long and narrow format, such as this three-panelled work, *Cross Section*, by Janet Twinn. Inspired by the autumn landscape, this forms one of a larger series looking at the cycle of the seasons. The imagery and colours of the fabric suggests sawn timber and the quilting features concentric rings, each ring marking another year passing. A similar format is used by an American member of the group, Dominie Nash. Inspired by the traditional Japanese scrolls used for mounting calligraphy, her screen-printed fabric with leaf images is used both for the mounting fabric and for the central calligraphy section, closely following the format and proportions of a scroll.

Above: *Cross Section*
(Janet Twinn, 2009).

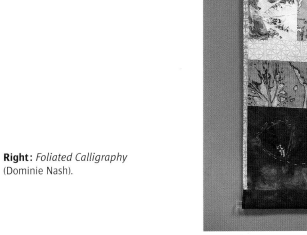

Right: *Foliated Calligraphy*
(Dominie Nash).

Communicating ideas

Collaboration can become much more complex when artists of different nationalities are working together, particularly when the collaboration requires two people to communicate their ideas to each other to create new works.

Since 1995, Lesley Millar, Professor of Textile Culture and Director, Anglo-Japanese Textile Research Centre, University for the Creative Arts, has been working in the field of curating exhibitions, concentrating on contemporary textile practitioners. Working for the most part in the UK and Japan, her explorations also include projects in Scandinavia and Northern Europe. Her particular areas of interest have been in textiles as intervention in the built environment, contemporary textiles that have emerged from a strong traditional practice, and those that reflect a particular culture. Through the Surface, 2004 (UK and Japan) and Cultex – Textile as a Cross-Cultural Language (UK and Norway) are just two examples of touring exhibitions from a long list, providing an ongoing international focus and resource for contemporary textiles. Her thoughts on collaborations are as follows:

Working collaboratively is rewarding but it is also hard: negotiating, finding points of connection, tolerating difference, maintaining the sense of self and creating a joint identity – what do you give, what do you gain, what do you lose? How much more difficult it is when the two partners in the collaboration are from different countries – as I have requested on several occasions. And if those partners also do not speak each other's language and have never previously visited each other's country, the difficulties would seem almost insurmountable. But not entirely – for cloth is universal, providing a material language connecting history with the present and one culture with another.

When textile artists Gabriella Göransson (Norway) and Kiyonori Shimada (Japan) were partnered by me for the project Cultex, both were, naturally, intensely worried about communication. Gabriella Göransson wrote in her online journal: 'It was really complete madness. Starting work with a person with whom I shared neither a common language nor a common cultural framework. And that the outcome of this cooperation should lead to a joint piece of work – the idea seemed increasingly more and more absurd.' However, precisely because they had no spoken or written language in common, they used their mutual understanding of textiles in order to cross cultural borders and develop the connections that would enable them to work together.

Such collaborations, when successful, can lead to long-lasting and fulfilling outcomes that neither party would have reached on their own. The partnership of Anniken Amundsen and Machiko Agano was begun in 2002 when both took part in the project Through the Surface. Over the years their discussion and exchanges have provided a rich and secure foundation for exhibition outcomes shown as collaborative installations. Both have approached their collaborative work in a spirit of openness, allowing their exchange to change their ways of thinking without losing their individual voice.

My experience has been that working together across cultures enables the identification of connection and difference to be developed and resolved through material outcomes, resulting in genuine creative exchange.

Lesley Millar

The works created for Cultex were site-sensitive installations which, while bringing artists together in collaboration, also interacted with people and with the exhibition spaces.

Machiko Agano normally works with monumental installations of knitted tensile curves and free-falling lines in various fibres, seeking to find a balance between the natural and the man-made. For Cultex, Agano used a technique new to her work: inkjet printing on fabric and mirrors. These, suspended in 'Greenhouse' alongside Anniken Amundsen's organic structures, woven with nylon filaments, create an atmospheric piece that explores issues of environmental change in relation to the development and conservation of human, natural and organic life.

Right: *Greenhouse* (Machiko Agano and Anniken Amundsen). Agano's photographs are suspended above Amundsen's organic woven nylon forms. .

Kiyonori Shimada created a breathtakingly beautiful white room in nylon titled 'Division' for Cultex. The cloth walls moved and rustled as people passed through, with 'windows' in the walls allowing glimpses of Gabriella Goransson's 'Out of Darkness', dark skeletal forms in fibre, climbing the walls of the gallery space.

Gabriella states:

I am not sure what I expected from the result in our two rooms. But something works – the dark, matt objects against Kiyonori's glossy, wavy nylon walls. The contrasts are obvious, though there is also a common keynote.

Left: *Division* (Kiyonori Shimada). Installation, with a view through to Gabriella Goransson's work, below). **Below**: *Out of Darkness* (Gabriella Goransson).

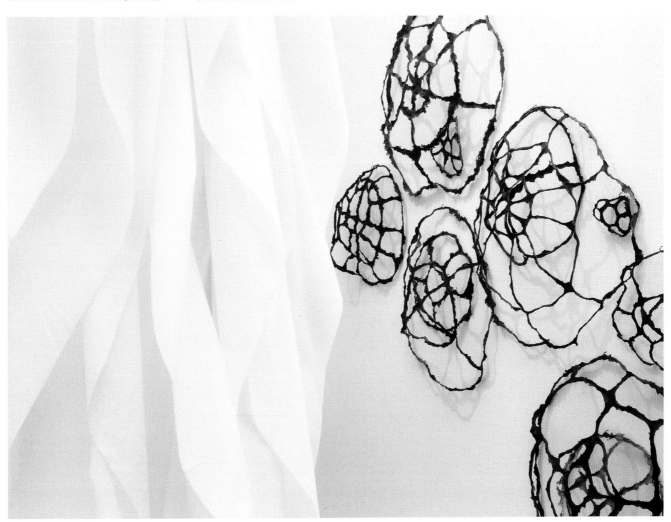

Research and collaboration in places and pieces, ceramics and stitch

Alice Kettle is a textile artist known for expressive embroideries which deal with psychological and mythological themes. She is interested in the variety and quality of lines and where line can meander and evoke a suggestion of narrative, connecting relationships between material, thought and emotion. Helen Felcey is a ceramicist known for delicate and distinctive unglazed bone china objects. She mostly explores cast objects, seduced by this smooth, formless substance. Working in a relatively 'permanent' material, Helen explores impermanent, fleeting encounters with the material world.

The two artists' collaboration came about through a joint exhibition designed to show the evidence of two specific projects. Helen had recently been to China, working at the Pottery Workshop, Jingdezhen, where she had produced a series of illustrated plates. Alice had completed a huge 16m (17½yd) wall hanging, commissioned by Winchester Discovery Centre as a permanent legacy. This work was required to be a visual narrative of place that confidently stated the creative outlook of a city and its sense of history. When the two discussed the shared exhibition, the stark

differences in these two projects were exposed, yet it also seemed to offer the opportunity to bring together two distinct areas of practice and two distinct characters. The idea for 'Place Settings' emerged through these very first conversations, when Helen expressed a wish to display her plates on a table and Alice simply suggested making a tablecloth.

Alice made Helen a landscape cloth that echoed the landscape on the plates. This required a sparseness of

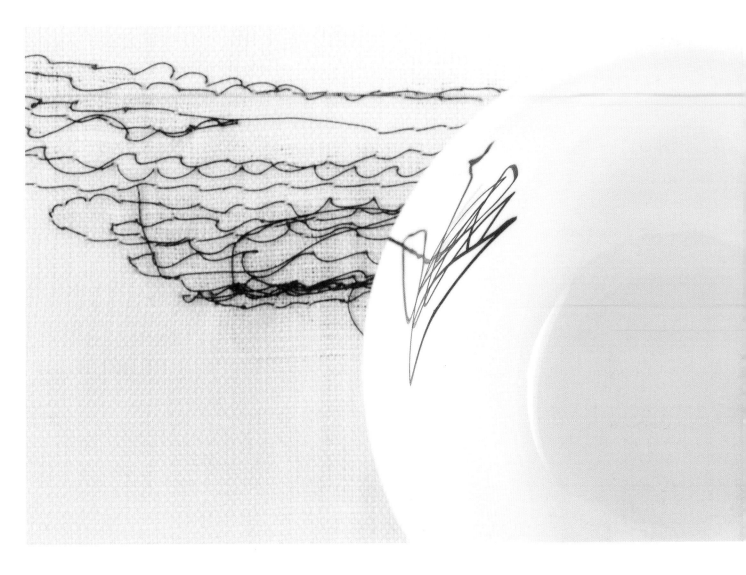

Left and above (detail): *Place Setting* (Alice Kettle
and Helen Felcey). Photograph: Stephen Yates.

mark-making and exploration into qualities of machine stitch
that had the openness and delicacy of porcelain, so neither
would dominate or overwhelm. For the first time, Alice left
the fabric naked and empty, so that tiny marks carried new
significance.

As the work developed, each twist of thread and thickness
of mark emerged as important. Alice then used basting and
fringe stitching to lift the thread away from the fabric and
embedded stronger tiny marks with a computerized fill stitch.
Alice's threads highlighted the fine meandering lines of red
enamel that appeared on Helen's plates and white pots. On
some occasions, these lines could be mistaken for thread; the
materials began to imitate one another. The unglazed, paper-
thin china casts appeared soft and malleable, the addition of

a single cotton thread tied around these forms furthering this
illusion. The thread introduced new tension to the forms. Each
time the table setting is laid out, a new set of associations
can be formed; while the components are similar, the changes
of positions and perspectives suggest a navigation of time and
movement.

To continue the metaphor of table setting, Alice made people
portraits to sit around the table. The figures appeared from
broken ceramic pieces, shards of broken pots – Helen's
seconds, enjoyably smashed for new purposes.

Underlying these actions was a sense of freedom and mutual
respect for each other's craft; an openness to respond and see
what happens, which created a new, rich space for practice. It
was to a good degree open-ended, and entirely about enquiry
and response – the process of understanding each other and
not making something complete within the parameters of
their own medium.

The written word as a starting point (Anne Kelly)

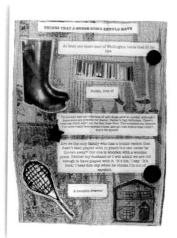

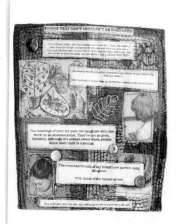
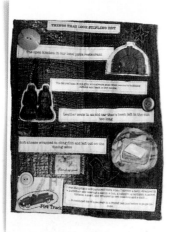

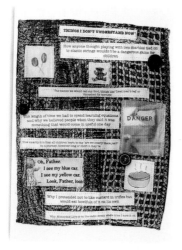

'Pillowbook', 2008, created in collaboration with writer Sarah Salway, focused on a series of embroidered-with-text artworks based on 10th-century Japanese author Sei Shonagon's Pillowbook. After reading the book, we identified passages with which we felt a connection, and Sarah then wrote a series of twelve contemporary interpretations. I choose to identify a colour that connected with each of the headings that Sarah had chosen and then isolated lines from Sarah's writing that could be interpreted in cloth, choosing imagery that represented them and using a colourful background as a base. Five finished pieces were reproduced as postcards and these were published by Sarah's press/imprint, Speechbubble. The original works have been exhibited in solo and group exhibitions in the region, the postcards providing interpretation and support material.

Sarah says that she had collaborated with other writers but

Working with Anne was very different in that it wasn't so narrative-based. Instead of 'what happens next?', Anne taught me to think instead about the underlying emotion. As a writer, I do think about metaphor and image quite a lot, but to see it happen away from words was really powerful. As well as story, I see my poems, stories, novels as a form of construction – putting one word next to another creates something bigger than two words. But having the visual references made it almost 3-D, and gave several more layers that I'd really like to keep on exploring.

Interestingly, Sarah makes reference to layers here, which I also use throughout my work. In conclusion, she also says

... as much I love art, I've always had an innate and uncontested view that text is the number one in terms of meaning. Now I'm not so sure! Here the value of working collaboratively can clearly be seen, and the feedback received about the finished work was overwhelmingly positive.

Right: *Pillowbook: Things I Think About But Which Are No Longer There* (Anne Kelly and Sarah Salway). Mixed-media textile on calico.

Left: *Pillowbook* (Anne Kelly and Sarah Salway). Printed postcard pack.

THINGS I THINK ABOUT BUT WHICH ARE NO LONGER THERE

The phone box on the corner of Claremont Road, from which I once made a call to say, *yes I would like to live here*

It's Friday, it's five to five and it's ... CRACKERJACK!

Mac Fisheries fishmongers, and its big bank of ice.

The plastic watch I won when I was seven for colouring a happy face on a tomato. The judges said it had the jolliest smile they had ever seen and I couldn't see what was funny when my dad said that maybe I had found my talent - drawing expressions on tomatoes

The greenhouse we used to have, and how I would hide in a corner to read my book but really so I could lose myself in the smell of hot geraniums

Curiouser and Curiouser: a museum collaboration (Cas Holmes)

'Curiouser and curiouser!' cried Alice (she was so surprised, that for a moment she quite forgot how to speak good English); 'now I'm opening out like the largest telescope that ever was! Goodbye feet!' (for when she looked down at her feet, they seemed to be almost out of sight, they were getting so far off).

Alice in Wonderland, Lewis Carroll, 1865

Above: *Corridor: Alice in Wonderland* (Jane Churchill).

To illustrate the story of Alice in a costume Wonderland, the Tunbridge Wells Museum and Art Gallery collaborated with set designer Jane Churchill, inviting her to create an installation using rarely seen objects from the museum's costume collection for inspiration, and incorporating the work of textile artists Heather Zeale, Anna Cocciadiferro and myself. Jane suggested creating areas within the space that changed the way the gallery was usually perceived; with tunnel-like corridors that wouldn't reveal everything to the audience in one go. She looked at changing scale, shrinking and enlarging spaces to reflect the scale of objects on display, giving visitors a chance to discover museum objects in new contexts. Jane cut forests of tree trunks out of huge 3m (3yd) tall dust-sheet fabric, creating light and almost transparent corridors for people to walk through. Costumes from 1865, the year that the book was first published, were used in the installation to illustrate favourite characters, including Alice, the White Rabbit and the Mad Hatter. Jane Churchill explains:

I wanted the audience to feel that same feeling of excitement and wonder that I did as I unwrapped unknown objects from out of their light, white tissue-paper wrappings. This really inspired my creation of the installation and informed my choice of materials for this magical imaginary world in which anything could happen.

In her design of the project, Jane looked at the practical and visual considerations. She met with the artists to discuss their work, aware that the installation environment had to give each artwork its own space. She also had to consider the conservation issues surrounding the care of museum objects. She adds:

'Curiouser and Curiouser' was a fine example of not just collaboration between practices, but also how artworks in response to museum objects could combine in a truly immersive and unusual experience.

Left: *Stitch Lace Cutlery* (Heather Zeale).

Right: *Armoury of Accessories* (Anna Cocciadiferro).

Textile artist Heather Zeale explains how the museum costume collection inspired her beautifully crafted stitched lace cutlery for the Mad Hatter's picnic:

I was really struck by the beauty of the handmade lace that adorns many of the garments. I wanted to explore how changing the scale of something so intricate and detailed would translate when enlarged. I used the sewing machine to abstract and draw patterns and, using a technique of layering fabric, stitching, cutting and burning, I have created a modern interpretation of a traditional technique steeped in history.

Textile artist Anna Cocciadiferro's inspiration came from tiny dolls' clothes, from which she took patterns to construct new works. In 'Armoury of Accessories', collected and fragmented antique specimens (leather, kimono silk, eggshell, sea shell and butterfly wing) are cleverly reconstructed to make a miniature costume that is also reminiscent of the anatomy of a shell-based creature. A second piece, 'Twister', was inspired by an unfolding dress sewn by a Victorian child as a sampler.

The fragility of bright jewel-like colours against the worn silk weave of the waistcoats in the collection reminded me of the transience of butterflies and moth wings, providing the inspiration for my pieces. I sought to capture this fragility in 'Lace Wings', long open paper pieces punched with butterflies, some breaking free from the strands, and 'Blouse', based on an old pattern belonging to my grandmother, which was pinned to the wall. This can be seen as a tribute to forgotten needlewomen as much as our need to seek out the unexpected, just like Alice, and be curious about the world around us.

Above: *Blouse* (Cas Holmes).

A project with Australian National Botanical Gardens (Julie Ryder)

Places of historical interest, museums and centres of learning can offer the textile artist exciting starting points for research, collaboration and exhibition. Julie Ryder, an Australian textile artist, brings a scientific curiosity to her collaboration with institutions. Initially, she studied and worked extensively in the areas of microbiology, haematology and serology, which continue to influence some of her textile work.

In 'artandthebryophyte' (2004–5), a collaboration with the Australian National Botanic Gardens, and organized through ANAT (Australian Network for Art and Technology), Julie worked with Dr Christine Cargill, Curator of the Cryptogam Herbarium at the ANBG. Throughout her residency, Julie had access to all the material she wanted, including the specimens in the herbarium and Dr Cargill's collection of SEM (Scanning Electron Microscope) images. She used these as well as her own images, taken with her camera and the light microscope, in the subsequent exhibition.

I made drawings and used the Library at the ANBG to research many of the aspects of botanical collection during the time of settlement. Because Dr Cargill and I worked collaboratively, we also started a blog in order to demystify the process of collaboration between an artist and a scientist and how we could create something from two seemingly disparate worlds.

Working towards the exhibition Generate, created to celebrate Charles Darwin's 200th birthday in 2009, further extensive research followed: '*I read everything I could on Charles Darwin for several months, in order to get a handle on what kind of man he was, how he thought and to what extent he was shaped by the society he was born into.*' The resulting artworks, made from a variety of media, hand-cut leaves, etched glass, tapa cloth and pollen, express ideas about Darwin's personality, his ideas and theories about evolution, and his passion for collecting botanical, geological and zoological specimens.

Right: *Generate: Emma* (Julie Ryder). Mixed-media, cut leaves on tapa (bark) cloth.

In November 2009, Ryder took part in a residency (supported by the Bathurst Regional Art Gallery and funded by Arts NSW) based in a cottage formerly owned by artist Donald Friend, and originally planted and landscaped by gardener Donald Murray. Ryder sought to explore the complex relationship between the gregarious, well-known artist and the reclusive, introverted gardener and, in particular, how she, in turn, could collaborate with their work.

I approached the artwork for the exhibition 'Companion Planting' in a different manner. I took fewer photos and made use of observational drawings to record my residency; I worked daily in the garden collecting plants to dye with and plant materials for works on paper. Nightly reading of the Friend diaries informed the text that was embroidered on to another series of cloths, giving insight into his relationship with Murray and his feelings of solitude once Murray had departed.

The works in the resulting exhibition, 'Companion Planting', are all dyed with plants from Murray's garden, and the organic materials used in the works on paper and small objects are also derived from the garden.

With this body of work, I have attempted to expand on the idea of 'companion planting' – where certain plants are grown together to enhance each other's performance – to examine the dynamics of human relationships; the struggle for identity and recognition that can occur between couples; the compromises required when one's desires and dreams do not come into fruition, and the bitterness that can fester under the surface as a result.

Right: *All My Days Follow All Your Nights – All Your Yesterdays are All My Tomorrows* (Julie Ryder). Mixed media.

3 Community Collaboration

Projects and Teaching

Both of us take part in community projects, through teaching and through working as 'visiting artists', roles that are not mutually exclusive. In our capacity as artists, we often collaborate on educational projects and in exhibitions, some of which have been described in the Resonant Textiles chapter. In this section, we look at other types of collaboration, providing practical guidelines for work in museums, schools and workshops, both here in the UK and abroad.

Communities and cloth

People getting together to collaborate in textiles has a rich history. Often, the makers of early works are unknown, even though their work is still appreciated. In times past, women readily got together to produce co-operative work at quilting bees. This practice was well developed in America, where Amish quilts were often a wholly communal product, as described in the following story, collected by Elisabeth Safanda.

A large group of women had gathered to quilt and in the course of the morning finished three tops. After lunch three of the women decided to walk home; en route they passed the house of a young woman about to be married. Finding no one at home, they walked in and saw the prospective bride's unfinished quilt on the frame. In three hours they finished the quilt.

Robert Bishop and Elisabeth Safanda, *A Gallery of Amish Quilts*, Dutton, NY 1976

Meanwhile, in England, social reformer and Quaker Elizabeth Fry saw the value of stitch as a tool for prison reformation, providing occupation in crowded prison cells:

Formerly, patchwork occupied much of the time of the women confined to Newgate, as it still does that of the female convicts on the voyage to New South Wales. It is an exceptional mode of employing the women, if no other work can be procured for them, and is useful as a means for teaching them the art of sewing.

Elizabeth Fry, *Observations on the Visiting, Superintending, and Government of Female Prisoners*, Norwich, 1827

Above: Two quilts with Canadian heritage. Left: hand-stitched quilt with text, made by Anne's Canadian grandmother in 1961; right: detail of quilt sent to families by the Canadian Red Cross during the Second World War, which belonged to Cas Holmes's grandmother.

The political power of stitch as a means for social change is not to be underestimated. The tradition of banner-carrying demonstrations had grown up with the Trade Union movement. These banners, with their combination of text and pictures, proved a source of inspiration for the Women's Suffrage movement, but there the similarity ends. Most of the trades-union banners were produced by professional banner-making firms established in the 1830s; the women produced their own, often collaboratively, and within the movement there was an arts and crafts society called the Suffrage Atelier. Most of the embroidery was worked predominantly in the suffrage colours of green, purple and white and represented strong leaders in the movement, its heroines. Beautifully embroidered texts were used to communicate their demand for equal rights and opportunities.

Opposite, top: *Under the Pomegranate Tree* (Anne Kelly). Mixed-media textile hanging with fabric transfer, paper and hand- and machine-stitched elements, based on a visit to Istanbul. Detail shown on pages 98–99.
Bottom: *Flags of the World* (The Charismatic Quilters).

Trades-union banners were silken, painted, highly polished works. Suffrage banners daringly combined embroidery, paint, collage and raised work in original and equally well finished products. Their effective use of mixed media was perhaps a result of the middle-class women's lack of professionalism – a positive outcome of 'accomplishment'. Decades of skill developed for ecclesiastical banners, altar cloths, drawing-room drapery and smoking caps lie behind the banners.

Rozsika Parker, *The Subversive Stitch*, Women's Press, 1981

This thriving interest in collaboration is evidenced in groups on a local, national and international level who continue sharing and exchanging skills and ideas in workshops, museums and schools, and in the home. As recently as 2012, the Quilters' Guild collaborated on 'A Gift of Quilts' and 'Quilts4London' as part of the events leading up to the 2012 Olympic Games. 'A Gift of Quilts' was a national project led by Jenny Rundle and Sharon Garrick, involving quilters of all ages and abilities, individuals and groups, villages and schools. Anyone who could hold a needle could share in the making of a patchwork quilt. These were then given to each country participating in the London Olympics and Paralympics in 2012 as a unique sign of friendship and peace.

One of the joys of patchwork and quilting is that it knows no boundaries. It is a truly international activity, and each country and culture brings something unique to the sewing table.

QGBI Handbook

Community curators at Tunbridge Wells Museum and Art Gallery (Cas Holmes)

The Museum and Art Gallery in Tunbridge Wells has a well-established programme of co-ordinating collaborative outreach and artist-in-residence projects and provides good working frameworks for artists working on museum collaboration. I have a long-standing relationship with the museum and have worked on three Community Curation projects. In its most recent project, mentioned earlier, which focused on the museum's extensive collection of textiles, the museum developed artwork with three different community groups, each working with a professional artist.

Artist Heather Zeale worked alongside a local primary school, creating pieces taking their inspiration from buttons and ribbons held in the collection. Anna Cocciadiferro, working on drop-in workshops at local community centres, created pieces inspired by the dolls' clothing. My focus was on the creation of 'textile butterflies', in conjunction with students from Meadows School, a local Barnardo's school. The project explored the theme of textiles old and new. Beautiful 18th-century embroidered waistcoats from the museum collection provided the inspiration and the children created simple three-dimensional butterflies and moths out of layered vintage and old fabrics. The pieces also incorporated student sketches, Photoshop designs and a variety of waste papers, including dress patterns.

Practical considerations

In projects that engage with the public, an important starting point is to establish the aims of the venture. Tunbridge Wells Museum described their aims as follows, but these guidelines can equally be adapted and applied to most collaborative community projects.

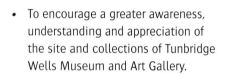

Aims of the project

- To encourage a greater awareness, understanding and appreciation of the site and collections of Tunbridge Wells Museum and Art Gallery.

- To give community members the opportunity to learn about contemporary art and craft through first-hand experience, working alongside professional practising artists.

- To provide links between contrasting community groups, with each other, Tunbridge Wells Museum and Art Gallery and the wider community.

- To make all forms of heritage accessible and relevant to a diverse group of people within the local community.

- To bring new and wider audiences to Tunbridge Wells Museum and Art Gallery.

- To support the creative industries and nurture the developing careers of young artists.

- To reach all community members in a way allowing for personal, creative and social development.

- To raise awareness of sustainability issues.

Left and above: *Butterflies* (Cas Holmes). Made with students from Meadows School.

With a fresh eye on the collections from Cas Holmes we found the combination of embroidered waistcoats and insect specimens, a combination we would not have suggested ourselves, worked very well. The students involved in the project enjoyed getting up close to butterflies and beetles from the collection, and then saw the link in the historic patterns, textures and colours they then used to create their own larger-than-life bugs for the exhibition. This approach certainly engaged their interest and changed their perceptions of museum objects.

Working with an artist in this way really opens your eyes to the possibilities of using museum objects as a source of inspiration. We never know what direction each project will take, so we are learning from the process alongside the participants and looking at objects in a new light. Once the work is on display, visitors can make connections between the original objects and the artwork, seeing details and asking questions that they perhaps would not in a traditional museum display.

We know from experience that projects like these make a real difference to the participants. Working with a professional artist, creating artwork in a very different, practical way and seeing that work go on show has a real positive impact on individuals and groups. It fosters a sense of pride and ownership that lasts far beyond the duration of the project. From the museum's point of view, this enables us to develop hard-to-reach audiences into loyal supporters.

Katrina Burton, Audience Development Manager

Above: Small stitched garments inspired by dolls' clothing (Anna Cocciadiferro), with Heather Zeale's ribbon piece in the background.

Below: 18th-century embroidered waistcoat from Tunbridge Wells Museum and Art Gallery (detail).

Methodology

The students had behavioural and related learning difficulties, so it was necessary to look at methods which could both engage and challenge them in relatively short sessions of 50 to 60 minutes' duration. I worked with the children, both on an individual basis and in small groups. We cut and tore fabrics and, using layering, pasted them together. When dry, these were then cut into butterfly shapes. This method could easily be transferred to your own shapes and themes. (This process is described in more detail in my earlier book, *The Found Object in Textile Art*, Batsford, 2010.)

The grid method

Materials
- Piece of plastic sheeting
- Paste or PVA and paste mix (diluted approximately 1:4)
- Fabric or paper base
- Selection of papers – parcel paper, wrapping paper, tissue – and/or fabrics
- Brushes, sponges and scissors
- Paper line drawing of your chosen subject (The example looks at using a grid, which can be worked on individually or in small groups, but any shape can be used, though simple shapes are preferable.)

Layering method

1. Draw a grid on fabric or paper; in this example there are nine squares.

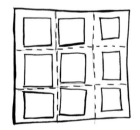

2. Cut squares out of your selection of papers and/or fabrics (or use other regular or irregular shapes) and place one in each square of the grid until you are happy with the design. Experiment with different colour combinations. Try to use no more than three or four colours.

3. Remove the pieces temporarily. Lay the paper/fabric grid on a piece of polythene and paint over it with the paste mix.

4. Add paper and fabric layers, using the grid for reference and pasting down each piece as you go.

5. Leave to dry overnight and then peel the bonded layers away from the polythene.

6. You can work further with the dry surface with printing and dye before simply machine- and hand-stitching the piece, to link your palette of colours.

Experiments

- Try different weights of paper and fabric – cotton, linen, muslin, brown paper, tissue or wrapping paper.

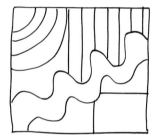

- Use different weights of thread and varieties of stitch.

- Consider using found items, such as bus tickets or seed packets.

- Quilt and pad layers.

- Use simple stencils, such as the butterflies, and cut shapes out of the layered fabric. These can then be further stitched or added to another surface.

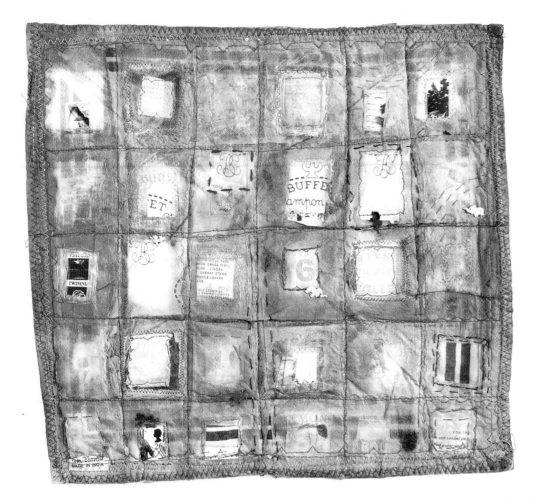

The following observations were made by a teacher supporting the project:

Metaphorically the theme of emergence and change has been reflected in the students' growing confidence and creativity as they participated in this project. Many young people who are unused to group work, socializing and taking responsibility, have contributed to the project. Some students continued to develop work in their own time and in other curriculum subjects. They also worked with new tools, methods and the medium of textiles, including using a sewing machine.

This is the first time pupils from Meadow School have been involved in doing artwork and exhibiting the work outside of the school. Working with Tunbridge Wells Museum has opened possibilities for students to achieve in spite of many difficulties they may have, proving that they too can have aspirations to succeed.

Sue Stilton, Meadows School

Often, requests for workshops do not come with a clear brief, and you will need to clarify what the requirements are. This can be done informally by phone and followed up by letter and email, outlining what has been agreed.

Tunbridge Wells Museum has clear guidelines and criteria in place for its artists and provided feedback as the project progressed. It is useful to make a simple checklist when organizing a community event and set up a simple project form. This covers the following:

- Contact details
- Description of the project
- Aims and objectives (curriculum, project ideas, abilities)
- Number, age and ability of students and whether any additional support is needed
- Location of the event
- Dates and times. How many sessions, over how many days?
- Space, facilities and other requirements for the workshop. Any restrictions to access by other users of the space?
- What fees are to be paid? Who is responsible for insurance? It is important that the organizer should establish that they have insurance to cover the project and is aware of health and safety requirements. (Professional artists should also have their own Public Liability Insurance.)
- Materials – to be supplied by artist, association or client group?
- Promotion, where relevant for an open workshop.

Upcycling garments: Bethany School showcase (Anne Kelly)

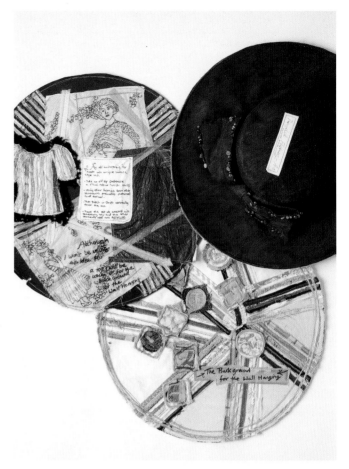

In a teaching environment such as a school or college, sharing skills and exchanging ideas with an artist provides a unique experience, exposing the students and teachers to different approaches in textile art and helping participants to develop new ideas and techniques as part of their coursework or learning.

I prepare students at A-Level for admission to Foundation courses and eventually to diverse careers including footwear design, architecture, fashion and textiles and interior design. My philosophy in setting up courses and teaching students has been to use and reuse materials. These are often donated or sourced through charity shops.

In the first year, students are taught basic textile techniques – silk painting, screen printing, batik, hand- and machine-stitching and embroidery. In the second year, students are encouraged to work to more personal and meaningful themes and explore them in greater detail. Materials can be shared and upcycled to create new and vibrant pieces of work, each with its own unique expressive personality and narrative – a jacket with a vintage feel uses a combination of text and photographs to describe feelings of separation and alienation; a mixture of dye and distressing techniques involves the use of a heat gun, as well as stitch, in the construction of the garment. In another work, charity-shop finds are placed on a background made up of torn and shredded discarded fabrics; accessory pieces are then attached over the top of the piece with heavy embroidery stitching. This is supported by a sketchbook made from an old hat. Another student uses an old shirt as a base for stitching, writing and illustration, exploring the theme of 'anger' and the colour red; the resulting mixture of drawing, painting, dyeing, stitch and screenprinting creates a dense structure of complex imagery.

Opposite, top left: Installation at the Royal Ballet School, London. Work by Amelia Mecklenburgh and Cathy Brown. **Top right:** Sculptural Wave Garment design by Helen Campbell.

Above right: Hat sketchbook for A-level coursework by Vanessa Ferdinands, Bethany School.

Right: Detail of upcycled shirt by Camilla Levett, Bethany School.

Showcasing the work of senior students is an important part of student development. Some of these students' work was shown in an exhibition marking the 50th Anniversary of the Society of Head Teachers held at the Royal Ballet School in Covent Garden in October 2011. This was organized by Alison Rhodes, Head of Art at Kings Ely School.

Eight independent schools participated, exhibiting a broad range of costume design, from sculptural installation work to more conventional evening wear. The exhibition was supported by a private view at which the Royal Ballet School performed, accompanied by the Purcell School and the Yeheudi Menuhin School. Guests at the event could enjoy the work on display and complimented those responsible on the high quality of work produced. It was good for the students and teachers involved to see best practice from other institutions. Giving the work a context and collaborating in a professionally managed event, such as this, encourages students to pursue their studies to a higher level.

Materials
- An old garment
- Images – transferred, drawn or printed on to cloth
- Scraps of fabric/remnants, ribbons, lace and buttons
- Coloured threads, scissors and needles
- PVA glue or heat gun
- Mark-making materials, such as dye, paint or textile pens

Step-by-step upcycling

Using your chosen garment as a base, follow the steps outlined below.

1. Distress, cut and tear your garment.

2. Stain or paint the fabric at this stage if you wish, and let it dry.

3. Place your photos and scraps of fabric around your piece, deciding where you would like them to appear on the garment. It is good idea to form your piece around a theme, looking at words, moods and colours.

4. Start with the main body of the garment and attach your images and scraps with glue and/or stitch. Glue should be used sparingly and applied with a brush or sponge. Ribbons, buttons, lace, transferred images and words can be added at this stage.

5. Once you have added the main components, it can be effective to add further stitching and embellishing, by hand or machine.

6. Add further marks with dye, paint or textile pens to enhance the decoration.

7. Finally, when your piece is dry, you can add further embellishment.

Kingswood School, Dulwich, London (Anne Kelly)

Teacher training in art is an important part of a teacher's practice. It offers the participants a chance to explore a range of art skills, from ceramics to book binding, printing, painting and drawing and, of course, textiles. At Kingswood School, Dulwich, I was invited to share best practice with textiles at junior level, and to observe some printing from an adjoining workshop. Taking world religions as a theme, staff and students were introduced to some basic dyeing and colour techniques for use on cloth and paper and some simple, adaptable stitch and appliqué techniques.

The focus was on circular patterns as they are represented in different cultures: stained-glass windows, mandalas and particularly Islamic patterns based on geometry. You can create your own geometric design using a similar process. The guidelines here are for circular designs.

A simple geometric design

1. Start with a blank piece of fabric and draw a large circle (or other geometric shape).

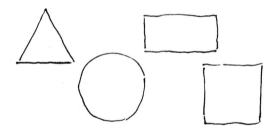

2. Divide the shape into sections, using oil pastels or fabric crayons to fill it with patterns.

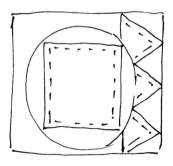

3. Colour the design with paint or dye. The oil pastels or crayons act as a resist.

4. Iron the fabric to fix the colour.

5. Embellish the design with stitch or beading to enhance the image further.

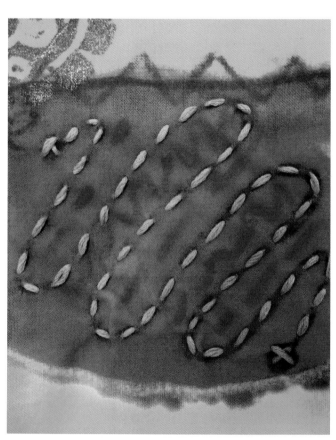

The finished pieces can be used in fabric collage, as part of a larger piece, or stitched or appliquéd on to clothing.

Constructivism to collaboration (Anne Kelly)

For comparison, more heavily worked stitching can be seen in the geometric pieces made in response to the work of figurative sculptor Louise Giblin, who asked me to produce a series of embroideries derived from her Constructivist drawings. She says, *'It's possible that it's my background as daughter of an engineer and an artist, and growing up in a marine construction factory, that draws me to related imagery and the machine aesthetic of early twentieth-century art movements such as Futurism and Constructivism. It seemed an ideal theme to me as Constructivism, an idealistic Russian movement...was founded on collaboration between the areas of pure and applied arts.'*

In 2008, Louise Giblin started revisiting overlapping, fragmented and machine-inspired imagery. Her series of work, 'Alpha Males' and 'Motor Heads', were created from the juxtaposition of portraiture and high-performance vehicles. Worked with heavily embroidered and textured surfaces, my four small pieces featured in the exhibition 'Body Casting Olympians', held at the Mall Galleries in London.

Above: *Constructivist Textiles* (Anne Kelly). Stitched panels in response to collaboration.

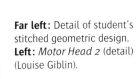

Far left: Detail of student's stitched geometric design.
Left: *Motor Head 2* (detail) (Louise Giblin).

Walk of Art: a primary project (Cas Holmes)

Balancing your approach as an artist with the needs of a participating group is a crucial part of the delivery of a project. In Walk of Art, a project with Bromley Council, students at Burnt Ash Primary School created a book, using textile and paper collage to reflect their walk to school. Communication, largely via email and phone, was a key element in organizing the project with both the school and council. A framework concerning the most appropriate approach to the project was clearly established; a timetable was agreed and it was decided which class groups should be involved.

As part of their interpretation of the locality, the children recorded their observations and ideas, and each kept a journal, 'mapping' individual routes to school. This also required the support of parents and helpers walking with the children. A series of line drawings was developed from their observations in the journals. These were combined with found materials and objects collected while out walking to create collaborative folding books and scroll pieces. Students, teachers and parents shared and exchanged skills and ideas on an equal basis in a project which promoted the benefits of the 'Walking Bus' to our health and indeed creativity (people observe more while out walking), as well as looking at the issues surrounding our 'carbon footprint'.

Drawing collaboratively

Different themes and ideas evolving through a shared drawing process could be applied to developing your textile work and are equally relevant to work you may do with others in educational projects. Ideas can be presented in the form of two-dimensional designs, three-dimensional forms or small folding books. The group drawing exercises discussed here demonstrate a typical approach, which can be adapted and applied to various projects and themes.

Materials

- A group of objects of a given theme or references as a starting point; these might be objects with reflective surfaces, small still-life objects or sections of existing drawings
- Large sheets of paper – preferably good-quality cartridge paper – though lining paper for a wall will do
- A range of drawing and mark-making materials
- Masking tape to hold paper down firmly
- Rectangular 'viewers' made out of card and a camera to isolate areas of interest (old slides or plastic windows from envelopes work well for this)

Collaborative drawing method

You may want to create some limitations around the drawing, such as restricting the colours and types of drawing material. For example, you might use only felt-tipped pens, charcoal and inks. Chunky wax crayons and large graphite pencils are good when working with early-years primary children, as they learn to grip and hold drawing media. The aim is to create a group drawing, with each person moving around the paper while looking at the objects. While drawing, work swiftly and try to capture the 'feel' of the object, rather than drawing precisely what you see in detail.

1. Each person starts at a given point on the paper. After a set time, change position. It is useful to move either clockwise or anticlockwise around the paper.

2. Make a second drawing in response to your new position and the materials and objects in front of you.

3. Each time a move is made, suggest another approach to making the mark, such as:

• Overlaying marks on another drawing

• Filling in the blank spaces

• Using a different tool for each drawing.

4. As you work, look through a 'viewer' for interesting areas and take photographs of the sections.

5. At the end of the drawing session, cut the drawing into sections and give a piece to each person to develop further ideas or designs from the pieces.

Drawing is an investigative process, and making further studies from collaborative drawing sessions helps to develop mark-making skills and abstracts the original references or subject. The marks you make can be translated into textiles, regardless of the medium you use, and also help to develop composition and ideas. Both drawing and stitch are tools for making marks and they can inform one another, developing new approaches in your work.

Opposite, bottom left: *Walk of Art* folding book.
Bottom right: Exploratory piece by Rita Brown.
Above: Folding book pieces made in a day as part of a teacher-training workshop at Middlesex University with the Making Project.

Connecting weave to stitch (Michael Brennand-Wood and Philip Sanderson)

At the West Dean Tapestry Studio, the dialogue between different textile media – the lace-inspired stitch structures of Michael Brennand-Wood and the strong shapes and subtle shifts of colour in tapestry weaver Philip Sanderson's work – created new narratives in mark-making:

The design for the tapestry was developed over a number of conversations about the possibilities of working collaboratively to produce a tapestry which combined ideas and techniques that we were both interested in exploring.

The design moved through a number of stages, from drawings and designs of strong colour motifs to a more restrained black-and-white palette with splashes and slashes of bright red. The design was also shaped by budgetary and time factors (the tapestry was woven in approximately three months, a relatively short time for tapestry).

The project created a great opportunity for the Studio to work in a less traditional way by incorporating techniques that engage more with the surface of the tapestry, such as wrapping and floating threads across the woven surface, which was crucial in successfully translating the fine lace areas within the design.

We spoke about the different qualities within the tapestry: the wrapping of warp threads using a bright scarlet rayon yarn to create a scar-like effect running across the tapestry (another first for the studio). This was worked in contrast to the flatter areas of colour and the dense blacks, which in some areas were given a smudged appearance by employing the subtle blending techniques we use when translating more painterly works.

The Space Invaders motifs were woven using a double warp, giving a relief effect and a softness to the image, complementing the parchment-like quality of the linen, cotton and wool threads used in the background.

The richness of the tapestry has completely transformed it from the original design, and the whole collaborative process has created a lot of new ideas for further works which both Michael and the Studio hope to develop in the future.

Philip Sanderson, Creative Director, West Dean Tapestry Studio, Spring 2012

Right: *Space Invaders* tapestry (Michael Brennand Wood and Philip Sanderson).

Teaching in Taiwan:
connecting cultures (Anne Kelly)

Collaborations are not limited by locality or place. When we travel, we are surrounded by fresh sights and experiences, which can be a stimulus for new work. Working and exchanging ideas with other practitioners can be a force for development and change in your work. Recording your ideas in a journal and through photographs helps you to retain your impressions and focus your ideas.

I ran two workshops with secondary students in Taiwan when on a student educational and cultural exchange between our schools. The first workshop referenced a scroll studied on a visit to the National Palace Museum in Taipei which depicted domestic plants and animals. The students, who were divided into two groups, were instructed to produce a mixed-media collage from their research drawings, using paper, fabric and found materials. The two groups were quite different in size and the results varied. All had some art training, but many had not previously done much or any collage or textile work. Using aspects of the materials they found interesting or colourful, the students added images, using stencils and paints. Torn or cut elements were assembled and pasted together with dilute PVA glue. Additional colour was added, using gouache paint for further paintings and stencilling.

The second workshop focused on 'everyday objects' drawn from observation. Selecting three objects from their pencil case as a reference, the students made drawings on good-quality cartridge paper. The drawings were altered by tearing or cutting and, using the same glue and paint methods described in the first workshop, they created a mixed-media collage. Some students chose to complete the work with stitch.

A preliminary demonstration ensured that the students were familiar with the techniques before they started to work, and they also worked on tester pieces alongside their main piece. Students focused on sewing through the layered pieces. As they progressed, the cultural differences and influences became more apparent in the work, along with a realization that we also shared some common interests. The results were impressive, as the collage enhanced the graphic nature of the drawings.

The work initially developed by some of the students led to a school project which was exhibited at Cranbrook Library Gallery, alongside pieces of our work following similar cultural themes. It was an opportunity for students to see their work in a public context.

Left: Taiwan sketchbooks (Anne Kelly [top] and Lydia Healy, Bethany School [bottom]).

Right: Work from exhibition at Cranbook Library Gallery by Bethany School students.

Textile workshop events: forums for exchange (Cas Holmes)

Textile holidays provide a fresh environment and the chance to meet new people as part of the experience of learning and exchange. At Studio Preniac, in southwest France, students on the course made drawings and rubbings and took photographs as reference materials, finding inspiration from visiting Vide-Greniers (the local flea market) and the local cemetery.

I like to visit graveyards when travelling, for a feeling of passed times and collective memory. I chose one drawing to make a print for the central image in my collage work. I wanted to represent the idea of historical layers that are, in a way, the essence of a graveyard.

Anita Toivonen

To connect the outdoor drawing to the textile, each person worked on similar materials at the start of the practical sessions, using a few of the fabrics they had bought with them. Marks were added to the fabrics with paint and dyes, paying attention to the existing patterns. After this, a selection of the materials were laid out into two collages, cellulose paste being used to hold them together lightly as a temporary fix. As the designs progressed, each person incorporated fabrics and papers that they might not have chosen to use but that were given to them by their neighbours. When dry, one sample was selected to keep for later work with stitch, while the other sample was used to practice machine-stitching methods. This second piece was then cut into a minimum of three pieces, a viewer being used to isolate areas of interest for potential compositions for small collages. Exchanging ideas can create a useful starting point for your own design work, as Anita describes in her working process:

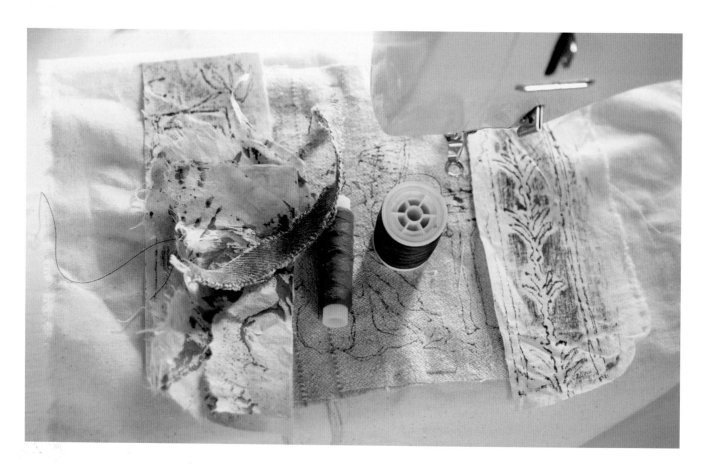

Left: Stitched stencil and print on cotton (Anita Toivonen).

Above: The completed sample piece by Anita Toivonen).

The resulting piece didn't look coherent and I realized that it should look more like scenery than a collage. I sketched a tree drawing and replaced the tree and flower cuttings with stitched trees. I felt a need to 'clear out' the odd pieces and make the picture look coherent. The process of undoing and reassembling was useful for it produced new thoughts about the subject of historical layers. Travelling to new surroundings for a workshop and meeting new people in the relaxed atmosphere of Preniac was a great deal of fun. The experimental process was very inspiring, giving me new tools and ideas, and making me experiment with techniques and approaches I might not try on my own. This broadened my expressive abilities and I discovered new approaches through observing other people's work, getting feedback and reflecting on my own work.

The process of assessing and isolating areas of interest in the textile samples for future creative exploration was returned to several times during the workshop. This practice can create a useful starting point for establishing compositional ideas and design themes.

Above: Anita Toivonen machining pieces at an early stage of the work.

International events

Many textile exchanges and events take place on a much bigger scale than a workshop such as Preniac and can include several tutors and events over a number of days. In the UK, the Festival of Quilts and the Knitting and Stitching Show have already been mentioned. Stroud International Textiles has celebrated contemporary makers in textiles since 2005 with its annual programme of events, which aims to broaden the perspective of textile arts and crafts to include art forms such as performance, dance, music and the written word. Quilt events and festivals are widespread. In the US, there are many local and national exhibiting groups and organizations, such as Quilts Inc, which holds the annual Quilt Market and Quilt Festival in Houston, which feature the 'Hands All Around' international quilt exhibition. Another large-scale event is the European Patchwork Meeting, which is held every September in Alsace. All of these events present opportunities for exchange, friendship and learning through exhibitions and educational work that profile textile skills and offer a wide range of workshops for all ages and abilities.

A resurgence of interest in craft techniques and textiles in the 1970s led to their use as suitable material for creative development and personal expression. In the United States, as elsewhere, this sparked an interest in the creation of textile study programmes (mostly weaving and other forms of textile construction) in colleges and universities.

The Surface Design Association (SDA) was founded in 1977, shortly after the first national Surface Design Conference, organized by Elsa Sreenivasam, (University of Kansas) and Patricia Campbell (Kansas City), was held at the University of Kansas (in 1976). With over 600 delgates to this first conference (three times the number anticipated), it was clear that there was a need for an organization to facilitate communication among artists, designers, scientists, students and teachers.

With an initial focus on surface-orientated work, such as painted and printed textiles, the SDA has broadened its focus to include constructed textiles, as well as surface techniques and embroidery. The SDA continues to hold conferences biennially in the United States, at different locations around the country. In addition, they produce a quarterly journal and have a strong web presence, with a website and regular updates on their blog and social networking sites to communicate and exchange ideas, skills and information with their membership. Collaborating on exhibitions is still an important part of the conference, as a means to showcase members' work. The 2011 exhibition 'Merge and Flow', included work from over 200 members, each of whom interpreted the conference theme, 'Confluence', in a piece measuring 30 x 70cm (12 x 28in), either vertically or horizontally.

Fibre Arts Australia (Cas Holmes)

The connection people have to cloth is captured in the Fibre Arts events in Australia, organized and coordinated by Glenys Mann. More than 200 people (mainly women) participate in these events, which happen in five states. Many of the women work and live in the more isolated areas of the vast continent, and this is a highlight of their year – a chance to be with fellow enthusiasts, exchange ideas and make friends.

Fibre Arts challenges expectations, stretching the concepts of textiles in a programme of workshops, talks and social events as well as 'happenings'. Well organized, the advance preparation is a testament to the wonders of the digital age, with updates and guides being sent to all participants and tutors interjecting with reminders I can only describe as an Australian take on things, such as to 'remember a warm layer' and 'did I mention to bring an extra pillow?', dotted through the to-do list.

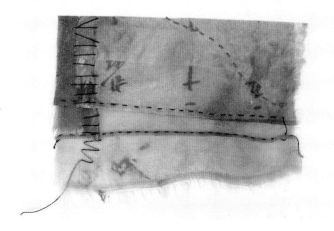

When I took part, the setting chosen for a workshop looking at the use of marks and layers in textiles seemed highly appropriate, as there was evidence of tracks and marks everywhere: vast lines of crops and track evidence of cattle, horses and people, the result of farming and management of the land, ancient marks etched into the rocks, scorch marks and cracks on dry earth or signs of new growth where water was present.

Using a small selection of materials exchanged within the group, we examined different kinds of marks, using paint and stitch to create richly layered surfaces. What became apparent as the workshop progressed was a distinct form of iconography in the use of symbolic and gestural mark-making that appeared as students worked on to cloth. The old and reclaimed fabrics and papers were stained, painted and scraped, and then combined with the edges of the frayed cloth and pierced with stitch. This strong yet sensitive handling of colour, texture and line had connections to the land, the rawness of the environment and its cultural heritage.

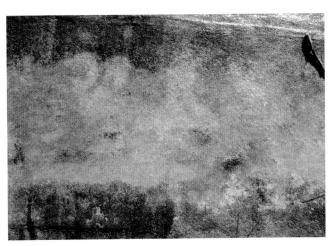

Left: Sample piece by Gail McDonald, with printed marks 'scratched' into the surface of dyed fabric and papers. These were then layered and machine-stitched with hand-stitching details, the straight lines echoing 'pathways'.

Top and centre: Two pieces by Meryl Graham using stained and dyed fabric combined with paper. The stains and simplicity of stitch reflect the marks on stone or in the soil. **Right:** photograph of weathered marks on stone.

Some of the students attending this Fibre Arts Australia event had just ventured into the world of fibre/textile art, while others had international experience as artists. This fertile environment for learning was enhanced by scheduled and impromptu events that happened throughout the week, from scheduled tutor talks to the organizing of a 15cm (6in) square textile exhibition and a silent auction for a cancer charity.

Outside spaces were also subject to textile intervention. The courtyard outside the dining room hosted a series of wonderful recycled paper-and-stitch sculptural multiples by Deb McArdle. Changing on a daily basis, the sculptures invited play and speculation about function as they interacted with space and people. Another open space saw a playful intervention by Dr Pamela Croftwarkon using plastics and found materials to create patterns reminiscent of textiles.

Connections between people, cloth and culture became a tangible experience in this exchange. Glenys Mann is a contemporary quilt maker working with 'found' cloth, namely old wool blankets and silk, all hand-stitched. The cloth is dyed with leaves, bark, lichen and other found organic materials. As with the energy and commitment she puts into Fibre Arts, the relationship people have to cloth is ever-present in her work.

The objects I make in cloth speak, shout, whisper and breathe in a language of silence. Their presence is tangible. I use found cloth because it has a powerful human presence and has the capacity to express humanity, human endeavour and emotion. Found cloth holds within itself the memory of all rites of passage, for at first and last we are bound by its weave.

It is as if cloth takes on the imprint of energy, the memory, of the body through the years of use and wear. Conversely, the body holds within a memory of that cloth.

Glenys Mann

In February 2009, bush fires ravaged the state of Victoria in what become known as 'Black Saturday'. Glenys's son and his young family lost everything in the fires. Within their very small neighbourhood, 11 friends and 43 houses were also lost. 'Memory Cloth #12: Numbers Lost' is a whole wool cloth blanket, dyed with plants. The surface is stitched with the markings of counting numbers, representing those lost in the fire.

Glenys descibes this work as a testament to the strength of character of human nature: '*It was like a way of getting my head around what happened, not only to our family, but to all of the 173 people that were lost and their families.*'

Left: Installation by Deb McArdle, featuring book pages bound and wrapped with red thread.

Creating new textile surfaces for stitch

Place a selection of papers and fabrics for shared use in a pile. These will provide a basis for exploration. Select a given range of fabrics or surfaces, such as:

- All-natural fabrics in neutral colours – cottons, linens, canvas, calico and so on.

- Coloured and patterned surfaces in paper and/or cloth.

- A mixture of natural and synthetic fabrics.

1. *Two pieces are given to each person in the group. Leave the rest for shared use. Divide each piece of fabric into three, and then paint or roll over the surfaces with a brayer or paint roller, using acrylic paint, emulsion, gesso or any water-based paint or dye you have to hand. It may seem like sacrilege to distress old fabrics, but working on them with painting and staining transforms the colour and textures and creates new surfaces to work with.*

2. *Look at how the different materials relate to each other. How has the paint been absorbed into the surface? Has the handling changed? Is it softer, stiffer? Choose additional fabrics from the shared pile, or exchange two of your 'new' surfaces with other people in the group for further experimentation.*

3. *You can use the stained and distressed fabrics to make stitched collage samplers or incorporate them into another piece of work.*

Above right: *Memory Cloth #12: Numbers Lost* (detail) (Glenys Mann). This piece records the losses in the Australian bush fires of February 2009.
Right: *Domestic Plastics* (detail) (Dr Pamela Croftwarkon). This piece, a textural play of pattern and lost objects, echoes the shape of a metal plate in the ground.

Between sea and sky (Mary Butcher)

Textiles' relationship with people and spaces is further explored in the work of Mary Butcher, who works mostly with sculptural basketry, employing the techniques of binding, weaving and stitching. Working in partnership with public organizations is a necessary part of her practice and includes an exhibition of East Anglian Basketry at Norwich City College of Arts (early 2011) and a residency at West Dean, where she also tutors. Working in collaboration with the local council and community of Odense in Denmark, she was one of 13 artists commissioned to create site-specific responses to a wild, isolated promontory, attached to the mainland by a narrow isthmus. Until recently a town dump, new landscaping has encouraged mixed public use, from walks and a skating park to use as a music venue. Mary needed to consider the scale of her work, its use of materials and its siting, so negotiating and planning with the local council and community was a necessary part of this collaboration:

The making involved hard physical work, but with a free discussion of scale, site, appropriate quality of weave and materials, with suggestions from others and with freedom to respond with small changes of plan. I picked a hilltop site for my 9m (10yd) piece, 'When the Boat Comes In'. Drilling showed the earth was compacted, so I moved to a mussel bed of local shells, a fine canvas for the willow and flags. Building was collaborative activity; Jan Johansen, a local maker and teacher, wielded the large drill and both of us shaped the poles and hammered them securely into the ground so they would survive the months of the exhibition. Weaving the willow to achieve a good height and visiting charity shops for the 200 or so flags of torn material, in suitable qualities of fabric and colours, involved Jan, Jette Mellgren, his partner and local basket maker, and several artists. The boat could be seen from the other side of the water on a fine day, so this scale was appropriate. The concept was mine but achieving it in the five days available made collaboration essential. The discussion and frequent review of both my work and that of others was stimulating and enjoyable. Local people often stopped to enquire, chat and tell us stories of the site and history of basket-making.

Mary Butcher

Mary discusses the importance of involving local people and organizations with the design process. This encouraged further interest and use of the space. Insurance and public safety issues restricted more direct involvement by local people, but this is not often the case with smaller outdoor projects. Working with schools and communities in outdoor contexts can provide exciting alternatives to classroom or gallery-based projects and also fosters connections with the environment, through practical creative work, observation and discussion.

General considerations when working outside with textiles

- Familiarize yourself with the space. What facilities are there on hand you can use? Do a risk assessment and all the necessary pre-planning with your group.
- Wear appropriate clothing and shoes; be prepared for wet weather. Bring food and plenty to drink as well as something to sit on.
- Allow time for talking, walking and getting to the site, collecting materials and tidying up. Most of all encourage quietness and take time getting to know the space.
- Look at the materials and resources to hand: available plant materials will be dictated by the changing seasons and elements. Are they appropriate or safe to use? Consider the effect of introducing alien materials, such yarn, plastic or wire, making sure there is no damage or distress to the surrounding area. Also make sure you won't cause an obstruction or any kind of danger to anyone or anything.
- Tools and equipment: you can manage with very little in the way of tools; at most, you may need secateurs, scissors, mallet, trowel and string.

As part of an ongoing commitment to outdoor art projects in King's Wood in Kent, Stour Valley Arts encourages school visits to look at both the sculpture and the environment in the woods. The pieces shown opposite were made in a one-day workshop with a local boys' grammar school, using the artworks in the wood as a starting point. The young people worked in small groups, sharing ideas to create textile-inspired sculptures. They used various different structural and attachment methods, while exploring patterns and geometric forms.

Outdoor textile techniques

- Weave into an open mesh. Roadside or garden mesh is brilliant for creating large-scale pieces when working with most ages and abilities. Think about scale and shape. Cut mesh into triangles, squares and other shapes. Weave, tie, lace and knot on to the mesh.

- Look at using materials in unusual ways and transform the scale. Crochet, knit with giant needles or finger knit, using plastic bags and fabric cut into strips. Tie, suspend and wrap fabric to sticks and branches.

- Look at creating simple geometric or textile-inspired patterns with leaves, wood or even found objects (working directly at ground level is ideal for younger groups).

Consider your location and the length of time the work will be outside. How will the weather change the work? Has this been factored into the construction? If you are using fabric, seams will need to be reinforced. Choose colours or materials that may provide a contrast and stand out. Working together, young people and adults alike will find quiet time to listen and observe the changing elements (effects of wind, rain, sun and time), as well as develop confidence in the handling of 'unusual' textile-making materials. This, in turn, increases our awareness of the connection (and the responsibility) we have to the environment (rural and urban).

The range of work created here involved all age groups and abilities and showed how collaboration can prove a useful method of exploring the current and historical uses of cloth. Working with textiles and related techniques in an educational context develops and reinforces the links between people and their environment.

Top left and right: Outdoor sculpture group project with Stour Valley Arts Project: geometric patterns with natural materials in the woods.

Above: *When the Boat Comes in* (Mary Butcher). Outdoor installation in Odense, Denmark.

Conclusion

The process of collating material, writing and editing has led us to pause and reflect on why we collaborate and the professional advantages collaboration can deliver. On a personal basis, we value the benefits of sharing ideas, skills and mutual feedback, and being able to contribute to projects we might not have been able to pursue individually.

Collaborations take place in many forms: in groups, between just two people, in larger organizations and even internationally and, while things sometimes do not run smoothly, the benefits of exchange can far outweigh organizational and individual difficulties.

Within the collaborative process, creative identity is important. Group exhibitions with a common theme benefit from the diverse approaches and ideas that can develop from a shared starting point.

Finally, collaboration gives 'added value' to your work:

• It forces you to be more critical and test your approach.

• It opens up new avenues and approaches to your practice.

• It demonstrates your ability to work with other people.

• It can provide new opportunities for exhibiting and working.

Collaborating is not for everyone, but working with cloth has a long history of cross-cultural exchange. Other writers have also expressed this:

Textile has a social, political and utilitarian history, moving across and between continents and peoples. It is a shared activity that stirs both conscious and unconscious memory. It is a language connecting practitioners in different cultures, as evidenced in their approaches and practice.

Julia Curtis, *Textures of Memory*, Angel Row Gallery, 1999

After considering the range of collaborations and joint projects described in our book, we have been touched by the stories and connections they represent. As Lesley Millar says in her book *Cloth and Culture*: 'These narratives are ones of connection, to the past and to the future, located in the present – the "now" of making.'

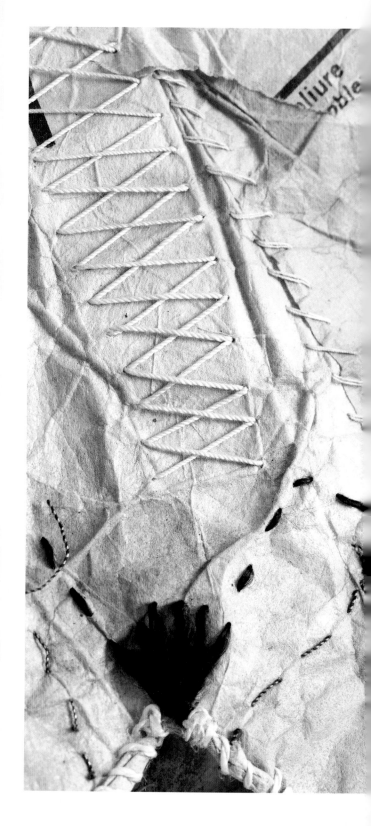

Above: *Blouse* (detail)
(Cas Holmes).

Right: *Whole Moth Tablecloth*
(detail) (Anne Kelly).

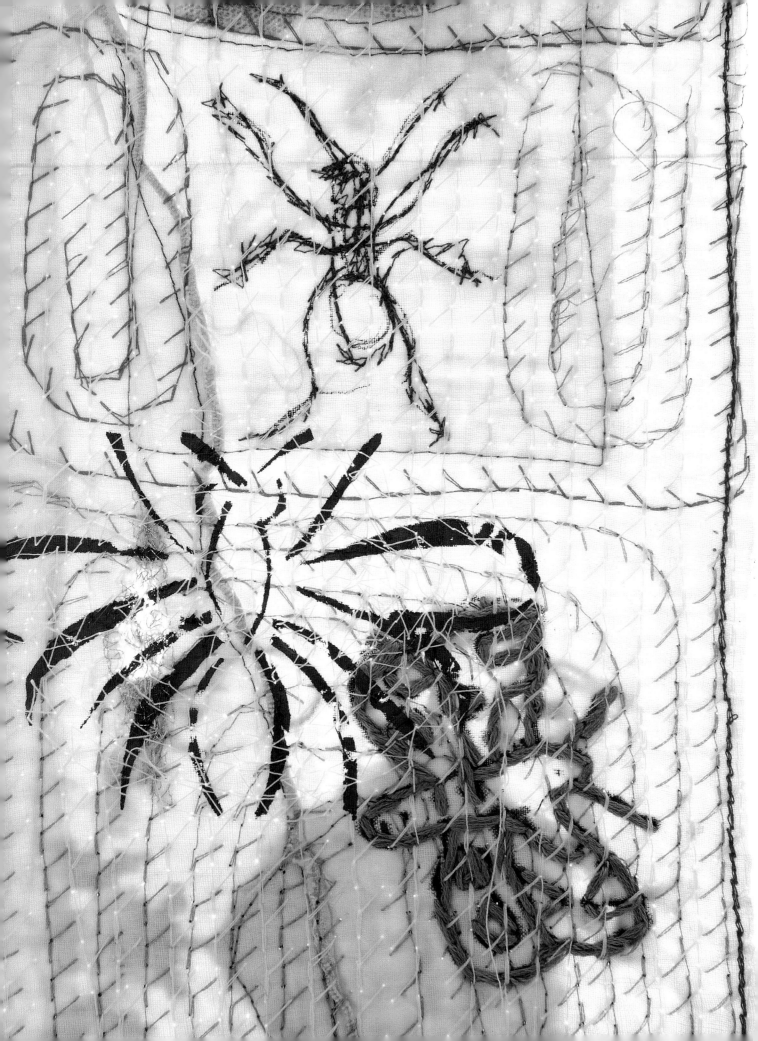

Suppliers

A major theme of our work is our responsibility to care for our environment and our philosophy is to leave a small carbon footprint. In addition to the suppliers listed below, it is often worth exploring your local art and hobby shops, as well as charity and second-hand shops. Use your local hardware and DIY shops for paint, glues, fittings and equipment. And re-use materials, whenever possible.

Textiles

George Weil (includes Fibrecrafts)
Old Portsmouth Road, Peasmarsh, Guildford, Surrey GU3 1LZ
Tel: 01483 565800
www.georgeweil.com

Rainbow Silks
6 Wheelers Yard, High Street, Great Missenden,
Buckinghamshire HP16 OAL
Tel: 01494 862111
www.rainbowsilks.co.uk

Whaleys (Bradford) Ltd
Harris Court, Great Horton, Bradford, West Yorkshire BD7 4EQ
Tel: 01274 576718
www.whaleys-bradford.ltd.uk

Winifred Cottage
17 Elms Road, Fleet, Hampshire GU51 3EG
Tel: 01252 617667
www.winifredcottage.co.uk

General art supplies

Art Van Go
1 Stevenage Road, Knebworth, Herts SG3 6AN
Tel:01438 814946
www.artvango.co.uk

Colourcraft (C&A) Ltd (manufacturers of dyes, fabric paints and Brusho and distributors of a wide range of materials including Markal Paintstiks and Koh-I-Noor)
Unit 6, 555 Carlisle Street East, Sheffield S4 8DT
Tel: 0114 2421431
www.colourcraftltd.com

Great Art
1 Nether Street, Alton, Hants GU34 1EA
Tel: 01420 593332
www.greatart.co.uk

USA and Canada

Pro Chemical and Dye Inc
P.O. Box 14, Somerset, Ma 02726
Tel: 800 228 9393
www.prochemical.com

Dharma Trading Company
Tel: 800 542 5227
www.dharmatrading.com

Quilting Daily
www.quiltingdaily.com

Australia

The Thread Studio
6 Smith Street,
Perth, Western Australia 6000
Tel: +61 8 9227 1561
Email:
mail@thethreadstudio.com
www.thethreadstudio.com

Above: *Garden Sketchbooks* (Anne Kelly [top] and Cas Holmes [bottom]).

Bibliography

Digby, John and Joan, *The Collage Handbook*. Thames and Hudson, 1985

Elinor, Gillian, *Women and Craft*. Virago Press, 1987

Greenlees, Kay, *Creating Sketchbooks for Embroiderers and Textile Artists*. Batsford, 2005

Holmes, Cas, *The Found Object in Textile Art*. Batsford, 2010

Howard, Constance, *The Constance Howard Book of Stitches*. Batsford 1979

Keble Martin, W., *The Concise British Flora in Colour*. Ebury Press, 1965

Kettle, Alice and McKeating, Jane, *Machine Stitch Perspectives*. A & C Black, 2010

Magnusson, Magnus, *The Complete Book of British Birds*. Royal Society for the Protection of Birds, 1992

Parker, Rozsika, *The Subversive Stitch*. Womens Press, 1984

Prichard, Sue, *Quilts 1700–2010: Hidden Histories, Untold Stories*. Victoria and Albert Museum 2010

Sterry, Paul, *Collins Complete Guide – British Wild Flowers*. Collins, 2008

Our Links

www.resonanttextile.blogspot.co.uk
www.casholmestextiles.co.uk
www.annekellytextiles.com

Group and Organization Websites

www.62group.org.uk, Contemporary British textile arts group
www.axisweb.org, artists in general, easy to use
www.canadianquilter.com, Canadian Quilters' Association
www.embroidererserguild.com, The Embroiderers' Guild
www.quiltart.eu, Quilt Art
www.texi.org, The Textile Institute, a worldwide organization
www.textilearts.net, an excellent website with links to embroidery groups, suppliers and exhibitions
www.quiltersguild.org.uk, The Quilters' Guild of the UK
www.sketchbookchallenge.com
www.transitionandinfluence.com, Contemporary Textile Arts Practice
www.twistedthread.com, Festival of Quilts and Knitting and Stitching Shows UK
www.wabisabiart.blogspot.com, a site about Japanese aesthetics
www.westdean.org.uk, full-time and short course programmes in textiles and other courses
www.workshopontheweb.com, Internet magazine for textile artists

Acknowlegements

The authors would like to thank the following:

Schools, organizations and named artists listed in the text, for use and creation of images and text

Sponsors of community projects and, specifically, Arts Council England and the National Lottery, who continue to support many of the community collaboration projects mentioned in the text.

Nicola Newman and the Batsford team for supporting this book.

Rachel Whiting, photographer.

Friends and family, for feedback and advice.

Picture credits

All pictures by Rachel Whiting, except the following: pages 18 (top left and right), 19, 22, 23, 26, 38, 41, 44 (top), 46, 50, 54–55, 59, 65, 68, 69, 71, 78, 80, 81, 95 (top left and right), 102, 103, 106 (bottom, 107, 108, 109, 110, 111, 115, 118, 119, 120, 121, 123 Cas Holmes and Anne Kelly; 20 © V&A. Photographer: Peter Kelleher; 63 Rob Kennard; 74 Eberhard Strabel; 77 (left) Els van Baarle; (right) Monika Schiwy; 82 Visual Photo Design, Netherlands; 83 Roland Hueber; 84–85 (right) Michael Wicks; 85 Gulezian/Quicksilver; 87 Kiyonori Shimada; 89 Lesley Millar; 92 © Speechbubble Press; 94 courtesy of Tunbridge Wells Museum and Art Gallery; 96 Derek Ross; 97 Rob Little; 101 David Matthews; 106 (right) Helen Campbell; 113 Steve Speller; 117 (top and bottom) Mika Toivonen

Index